LEVEL 1
Text Production & Word Processing

Sharon Spencer

Endorsed by OCR for the Certificates in Text Processing

www.heinemann.co.uk
✓ Free online support
✓ Useful weblinks
✓ 24 hour online ordering

01865 888058

Heinemann
Inspiring generations

Heinemann is an imprint of Pearson Education Limited, a company incorporated in England and Wales, having its registered office at Edinburgh Gate, Harlow, Essex, CM20 2JE. Registered company number: 872828

Heinemann is the registered trademark of Pearson Education Limited

© Sharon Spencer 2004

First published 2004

09
10 9 8 7 6 5

British Library Cataloguing in Publication Data is available from the British Library on request.

ISBN 978 0 435453 66 4

Typeset by Techtype, Abingdon, Oxon
Printed by Ashford Colour Press Ltd, Gosport, Hampshire

Tel: 01865 888058   www.heinemann.co.uk

Contents

Introduction

In today's workplace it would appear that many staff are now expected to produce their own correspondence and do not have access to a secretary or word processor operator. Learning to keyboard and to be able to produce professional looking documents is therefore becoming more important.

If you have to produce your own documents at work, then it is so much more efficient if you can key in text accurately and quickly. If you can produce professional looking documents then this will reflect well on your overall performance. The skills you will learn from this book should serve you well, not just in the examinations but also in the workplace.

About this book

The aim of this book is to provide a step-by-step guide to producing the documents required for each of the following two examinations offered by OCR Examinations Board at Intermediate Level.

Text Production
Word Processing

The main features are:

- A step-by-step guide to using Word to create each of the documents required for the examinations.
- Essential English skills to ensure that you produce well-written documents that do not contain grammatical or punctuation errors.
- Consolidation practice for each task to ensure you have thoroughly learned and understood the instructions.
- Examination practice to ensure you are thoroughly prepared for the examination tasks.
- Useful sections on common errors and how to resolve them.
- Recall text provided on CD to use with the exercises for Word Processing.
- Worked examples of all exercises contained in the book. These are provided on the CD.

The book is divided into 3 sections:

Part 1 – Essentials of using Word

This section gives you the basic knowledge to be able to key in text and format documents. You will learn how to save and print your material. These skills are required before you can move on to the examination material.

Part 2 – Text production

This section covers all the knowledge and skills you will require in order to take and pass the Text Production examination at Level 1 (Intermediate). It includes theory and practice exercises on business letters, memos and articles. A consolidation section will help you become familiar with the examination layout. This is followed by a common errors section which will show you the type of errors commonly made in the examination – and how to resolve them. The examination practice contains full length examination style pieces for you to complete within the 1 hour 15 minutes allowed for the examination.

Part 3 – Word processing

This section covers all the knowledge and skills you will require in order to take and pass the Word Processing examination at Level 1 (Intermediate). It includes theory and practice exercises on articles, notices, tables and business letters and memos. A consolidation section will help you become familiar with the examination layout. This is followed by a common errors section which will show you the type of errors commonly made in the examination – and how to resolve them. The examination practice contains full length examination style pieces for you to complete within the 1 hour 30 minutes allowed for the examination.

A CD is also provided for your use and contains the following:

Recall text

The Word Processing examination requires you to recall text saved on disk or the hard drive of your computer. These files are then added to and amended as part of the examination. The CD which accompanies this book contains all the recalled text required for the Word Processing examination.

Worked examples

A worked copy of each exercise is provided on CD. When you have completed an exercise, check your version with the version contained on the CD. You can either print these or view them on screen, whichever you find easier.

Part 1

Essentials of using Word

This section shows you the essential basics of using Word. You will need to be able to do all of the items listed below before you can start to work on the examination tasks.

Included in this part is information on:

- Loading Word
- Formatting documents 1
- Proofreading
- Printing and saving documents
- Proofreading – using the spellchecker facility
- Capital letters
- Setting tabs
- Accessing the Help function
- Formatting documents 2

Loading Word

In this section you will learn about:

- loading Word
- changing the document view
- toolbars and menus

To open Word you will need to be in Windows. How you load Windows will depend on whether you are using a networked or stand-alone system.

Exercise 1.1

1 Find out whether you are using a networked or stand-alone system.
2 Find out how to load Windows on your system.
3 Load Windows.

Once you have loaded Windows you will see the 'desktop'. This is the main menu from which you move around in Windows. It will look something like Figure 1.1, but the icons may differ according to the programs installed and the setup options that have been defined.

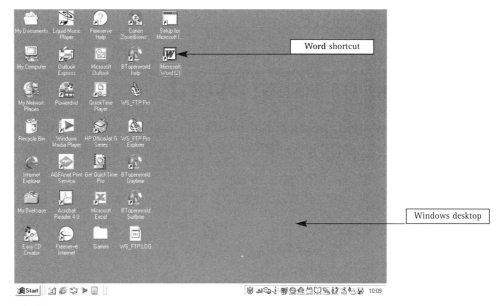

Figure 1.1 Windows desktop

Once you have reached the desktop you will be ready to open Word. You may see a shortcut icon on the desktop which will take you straight to the Word software. If the icon is not on the desktop then you will need to open Word from the **Program** menu using the **Start** button.

Exercise 1.2

Load Word.

Method 1

1 Move the mouse cursor over the **Start** button and click the left mouse button. A pop-up menu will appear listing the various programs and applications installed on the computer (see Figure 1.2).

Figure 1.2 Loading Word using the **Start** button

2   Highlight **Programs** by moving the mouse over it and another menu will appear.

3   **Drag** the mouse across to **Microsoft Word** and click on it. Word will now begin to load.

Method 2 (Use if you have a shortcut icon to Word on your desktop)

1   Click on the **Microsoft Word** shortcut icon (see Figure 1.3).

Figure 1.3 Word shortcut icon

You will be taken to a blank document on which you can start working. The screen should look like Figure 1.4 below. Note, however, that the view used here is called **Print Layout**. If you are not using this view then the page will be different.

Figure 1.4 Blank document

Exercise 1.3

Change the view to Print Layout, or look at the various views available.

Method 1

1   Go to <u>V</u>iew on the toolbar and choose **Print Layout** from the choices available. (If you cannot find **Print Layout** then click on the arrow at the bottom of the menu. This will now expand and show all the choices available.)

2   Click on **Print Layout**. If your default setting is **Print Layout** then choose a
different view such as **Normal** or **Outline**. Notice the difference in layout.

| Normal | Web | Print | Outline |

Figure 1.5 View menu

Toolbars and menus

The desktop in Word displays a variety of toolbars and menus. Look at Figure 1.6
below. Your screen may not look the same as Figure 1.6 – it may be displaying more
or fewer toolbars. This is because you are able to customise the toolbars displayed in
Word. In Figure 1.6 a large number of toolbars are displayed so that easy access is
provided to the various tools available.

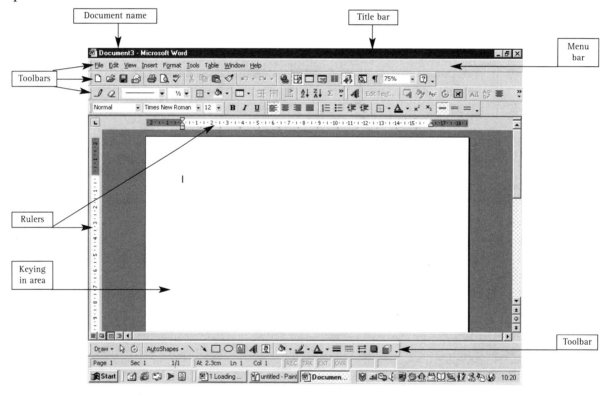

Figure 1.6 Word desktop

Formatting documents 1

It is important to format your documents correctly so that your work looks neat and tidy. This means that your margins are correctly set, the page orientation is correct and that you use the same font style and size throughout the main body of the text.

If you take care to format your documents correctly your work will have a professional feel to it.

Before you start keying in text you should be able to set the following in Word to ensure your document is correctly formatted:

- Paper size and orientation
- Margins
- Font type and size
- Line spacing
- Line endings

Paper orientation

The paper size required for most documents is A4, which measures 210 × 297 mm. Look at Figure 1.7 below.

Portrait orientation
(Shortest edge at top)

Landscape orientation
(Longest edge at top)

Figure 1.7 A4 paper

You will note that there are two ways of using the paper – portrait and landscape. Portrait has the shortest edge at the top and landscape has the longest edge at the top. It is important that you remember these and use them correctly.

To ensure that Word recognises the correct paper size for your document, you can check the settings by using the following method.

Exercise 1.4

Check the paper size and orientation of your document.

Method

1   Go to **File** and choose **Page Setup**.
2   The following menu will appear (see Figure 1.8).

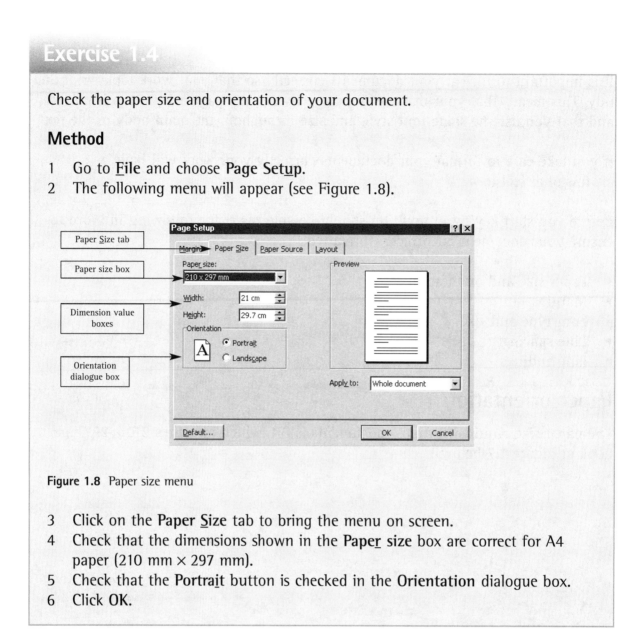

Figure labels:
- Paper Size tab
- Paper size box
- Dimension value boxes
- Orientation dialogue box

Figure 1.8 Paper size menu

3   Click on the **Paper Size** tab to bring the menu on screen.
4   Check that the dimensions shown in the **Paper size** box are correct for A4 paper (210 mm × 297 mm).
5   Check that the **Portrait** button is checked in the **Orientation** dialogue box.
6   Click **OK**.

Margins

The margins relate to the space around the text in a document. In Word, the default margins (that is those pre-set by the software package) are as follows:

Top	2.45 cm
Bottom	2.45 cm
Left	3.17 cm
Right	3.17 cm

These give a reasonable amount of space around the text, making the page easy on the eye. You can, of course, adjust the margins and this is particularly useful if you want to fit just one line of text at the bottom of a page. However, you must be aware that most printers will not allow printing less than 0.5 cm from the edges of the paper.

Exercise 1.5

Change the margins to 3 cm top and bottom and 4 cm left and right.

Method

1 Go to **File** and choose **Page Setup**.
2 The following menu will appear (see Figure 1.9).

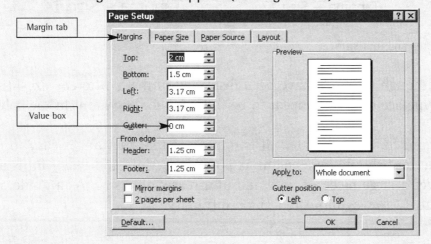

Figure 1.9 Page Setup menu

3 Ensure the tab entitled **Margins** is uppermost, if not click on it.
4 Click in the **Value** box for the **Top** margin. Either double click so that the existing value is highlighted or drag the cursor to highlight the existing value. Key in 4 cm. Alternatively, use the arrow boxes to the right of the Value box to adjust the margin in small units.
5 Repeat the steps for the **Bottom, Left and Right** margins.
6 When you have completed all the boxes click **OK**.

Font

The typeface of a document is called the font. You should ensure that you are using a suitable font for your document, one that is easy to read and is neither too large nor too small.

In the workplace your company will probably dictate the font that is to be used for documents as part of its 'house style'. House style means the standard layout, font, size, and other formatting items that are used for all documents throughout the business.

Look at Figure 1.10 below to see some different fonts and sizes.

Times New Roman – Size 10	Times New Roman – Size 12	Times New Roman – Size 14
Arial — Size 10	Arial — Size 12	Arial — Size 14
Ryans Hand – Size 10	Ryans Hand – Size 12	Ryans Hand – Size 14
Comic Sans - Size 10	Comic Sans - Size 12	Comic Sans - Size 14
Garamond – Size 10	Garamond – Size 12	Garamond – Size 14
Tahoma – Size 10	Tahoma – Size 12	Tahoma – Size 14

Figure 1.10 Different fonts and font sizes

You can see that although the fonts have been displayed in three different sizes, the actual size of the typeface does not appear to be the same for each font in the column.

When choosing a font for a piece of text it is important that the font is easy to read. This means that the font should be as plain as possible (scripts and fancy fonts are difficult to read over a large piece of text) and of a reasonable size. As a guide, most people can read size 12 font without too much difficulty.

Exercise 1.6

Change the style and size of the font.

Method 1

1   Go to **F**o**rm**at on the menu bar and choose **F**ont. The following menu will appear (Figure 1.11).

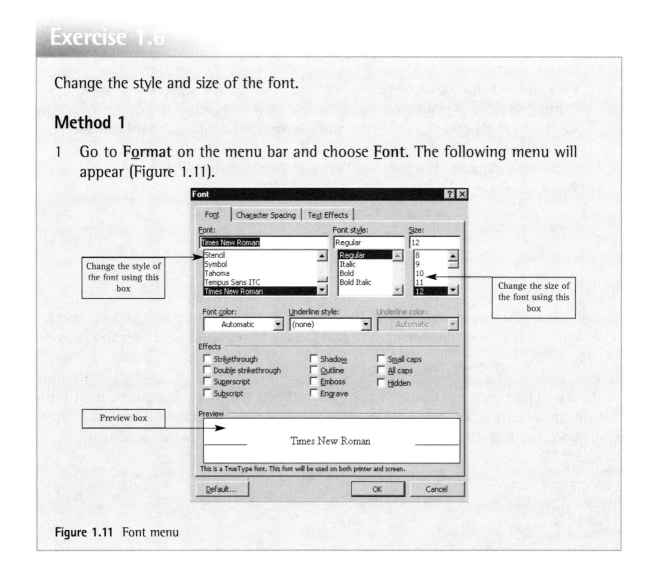

Figure 1.11 Font menu

2   To change the style of the font, use the arrows at the right-hand side of the **Font** box to scroll through the styles available. When you have found a suitable font, click on the name. The name should then change in the **Preview** box.

3   To change the size of the font, use the arrows at the right-hand side of the **Size** value box until you find the correct size and click on the number. The size of the text shown in the **Preview** box should change.

4   When you have finished making the amendments, click on **OK** to confirm your choice(s).

Method 2

1   On the toolbar you will find the **Font** and **Size** value boxes (see Figure 1.12 below).

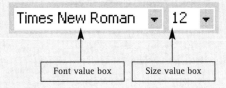

Figure 1.12   Font and Size value boxes

2   Click on the arrow next to the **Font** box and a drop-down menu showing the various fonts available will appear. Using the arrow, scroll down until you find a suitable font. Click on the name. The name will now change in the Value box. Repeat the same steps for the size.

Line spacing

Line spacing is the term given to the white space that appears between the lines of text. Look at Figure 1.13 below.

Single line spacing is the most widely used form of spacing. It is particularly appropriate for business letters and memos. There are no clear line spaces between the lines of text.

One and a half line spacing gives a half line of clear white space between the lines of text. This is useful for drafts and reports.

Double line spacing has spacing of a clear line between lines of text. This means that the space between the two lines of text is equal to that of one line of text.

Figure 1.13   Line spacing

You will use single line spacing for letters and memos, however you may be asked to draft work in one and a half or double line spacing. To set the line spacing, do the following:

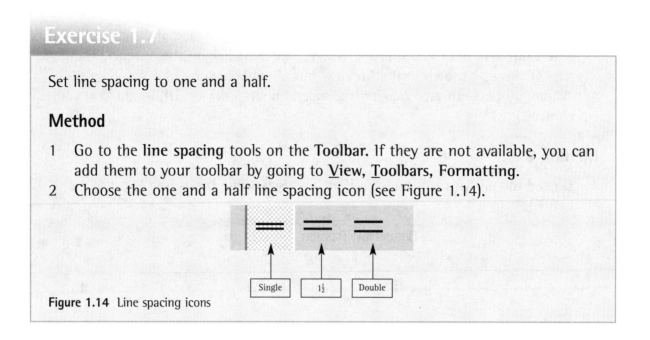

Exercise 1.7

Set line spacing to one and a half.

Method

1 Go to the **line spacing** tools on the **Toolbar.** If they are not available, you can add them to your toolbar by going to **View, Toolbars, Formatting.**
2 Choose the one and a half line spacing icon (see Figure 1.14).

Figure 1.14 Line spacing icons

Line endings

When you are keying in text you do not need to press the **enter** key at the end of each line. If you just keep typing, the text will automatically go onto the next line. This is called **Text Wrap.** You should only use the **enter** key to take you to a new line for the following:

- Items in lists or bullets
- Spaces between paragraphs
- Spaces between headings.

Exercise 1.8

Key in the following text using one and a half line spacing. A worked example of this exercise can be found on the CD-ROM.

Care of Jewellery

If you would like your jewellery to keep sparkling you will need to treat it carefully and clean it on a regular basis.

Cleaning jewellery should be approached cautiously as some modern cleaning materials can damage the stones. In the first instance, try brushing the item with a clean, soft paintbrush. This will remove any loose surface dirt.

Check that the stones are securely set in the mount. Remember that some stones are set with glue. Liquid cleaners should not be used for these items as this may loosen the setting. If you are in any doubt, then take your piece to a reputable jeweller. If the stone needs securing they will be able to do it professionally.

One of the main causes of dull, lifeless stones is hard water. If you live in a hard water area then take off any rings or bracelets before immersing your hands in water.

If the stones have already been affected by hard water deposits, then clean with a small amount of distilled water and diluted washing-up liquid. Use a small paintbrush to apply the solution. Dry very thoroughly with a lint-free cloth.

Proofreading

This is probably the most important part of any text processing examination and, in fact, of producing documents in the workplace. Many people believe that the skill involved in learning to keyboard is all about the speed at which you can type. This is only part of the skill. The really important thing is to be able to keyboard quickly and accurately. There is no point in being able to keyboard quickly if your work is full of errors. Equally, if you are employed to key in documents, then your employer will want you to produce documents at a reasonable rate of production.

Unfortunately, we are not always able to spot our own mistakes easily. This means that you have to take the time and trouble to read your work very carefully, either on screen or with a printed copy, and amend your errors before producing a final copy. It helps tremendously if, when you are reading your work, you make sense of the text you are keying in. This makes spotting errors much easier as any incorrect words should leap out at you.

The most common errors include:

- Typographical errors – these are pure keying in mistakes, eg *plase* instead of *please*
- Incorrectly spelt words, eg *proffeshional* instead of *professional*
- Words used in the wrong context, eg are/our
- Punctuation and grammar errors
- Words and/or sentences omitted.

Exercise 1.9

Check the work you have just keyed in very carefully. Did you find many errors?

Printing and saving documents

In this section you will learn about:

- printing documents
- saving documents
- exiting Word

Printing your work

Exercise 1.10

Continue using Exercise 1.9. Correct any errors you may have found. Print a copy of this document.

Method

1   Go to **File**, choose **Print**. The following menu will appear (Figure 1.15).

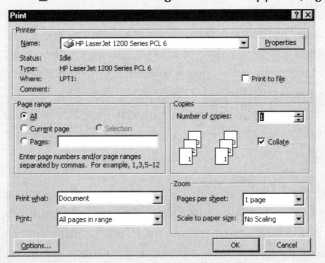

Figure 1.15   Print menu

2   In the **Page range** dialogue box, ensure that the correct pages are selected. For this exercise, the default setting of **All** is fine.
3   In the **Copies** dialogue box, ensure that the number in the **Number of copies** value box is set at 1.
4   Click **OK**.

Note: The print menu may vary depending on the type of printer you are using and, if you are using a networked PC, the network settings.

Saving your work

You will need to save the documents you produce so that they can be retrieved at a later date. It is a good idea to save your work as often as possible. This will ensure that if anything goes wrong, such as the computer crashing, your work will not be totally lost.

To save your work, do the following:

Exercise 1.1

Save the document as 'Jewellery'.

Method

The first time you save a document you will need to give it a name. After that you just need to save the work, usually without renaming it.

1   Go to **File** and choose **Save As**. The following menu will appear (Figure 1.16).

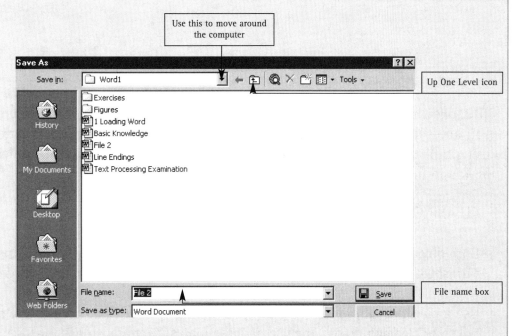

Figure 1.16 Save As menu

2   If the name of the folder in which you are going to save the work is on screen, then double click on the name to open it.
3   If the name of the folder in which you are going to save the work is not on screen then you will need to find it. You can do this by clicking on the arrow shown in Figure 1.16. This will show you the various components on the computer, such as the hard drive, a floppy drive (to take discs) or a CD drive. Click on the correct one and then using the same method move around to find the folder you want.
4   You may also use the **Up One Level** icon which will move you around the existing folders and then the computer elements.

> 5 Once you have found and opened the correct folder, make sure the cursor is flashing in the **File name** box. Key in the name of the document – for this exercise use 'Jewellery'.
>
> 6 Click the **Save** button to save your work.

Exiting Word

Practise closing down and exiting Word.

Exercise 1.12

Close down and exit Word.

Method

1 Ensure you have saved your work using the method given above.
2 Go to **File** and choose **Exit**. Word will now shut down safely.

Exercise 1.13

The following exercise contains a number of errors. See if you can find them. When you have finished proofreading the document, load Word and key in a correct copy using a blank document and double line spacing. The answers to this exercise can be found in the worked examples on the CD-ROM.

CLEANING GOLD AND SILVER

Both golde and silver will dull with connstant ware. Silver may, in time, become tarnished. The following hints will help you keep your jewelllery in mint condition.

Use a polishing clothe to give a shine to metals. You will not need to use any polish or cleaning fluids. The use of these may afffect any stones that are mounted in the
the piece.

Store silver in a coool, dry place and preferebly in an airtight box. This will help prevent tarnishing. Wood often contains acid's that may affect the surrface of silver. For this reason, doe not leave silver jewellery directly on a wooden surface.

As with all jewellery, avoid overexposure to artificial light or sunlite.

Proofreading – using the spellchecker facility

Word has a spellchecker facility that can help you find spelling and typographical errors. However you should not rely entirely on the spellchecker as it will not pick up the following errors:

- If you use an incorrect but real word, for example if you key in cheque instead of check.
- If you are keying in names and addresses, or technical words.
- If you omit a word or sentence.

The English language contains many words that sound the same but mean different things and are spelt in different ways. Take 'sew' for example. Spelt this way it means to stitch. Spelt 'sow' it means to plant seeds, but also, depending on the pronunciation, it can mean a female pig. To add to the confusion we also have the word 'so'. The spellchecker has no way of knowing the context in which you are using the word and it would mark any of these as correct.

To use the spellchecker facility do the following:

Exercise 1.14

Key in the following document and then use the spellchecker to find any errors.

> It wood bee nice to sea the see from time to time. I love the waves and the noise that the see makes. Won can never be sure what the see is going to be doing next. Watching the boats sale buy is also very relaxing. Whenever possible, I like to spend a weak or sow at the beech. The seens are fantastic and it is interesting watching others enjoy themselves on there holidays.

Method

1 Check the text you have keyed in against the exercise to ensure that nothing has been missed.
2 Ensure that the cursor is flashing in the text. Go to **Tools** and choose **Spelling**. Alternatively, press **F7**. The spellchecker will automatically check your document. Unless you have made any typographical errors the spellchecker should not find any mistakes in the text you have just keyed in.
3 If you have made an error, check the options you are given (see Figure 1.17). Choose the correct option – be careful here as the correct option is not always the first option. To choose an option, click on the word you wish to use.

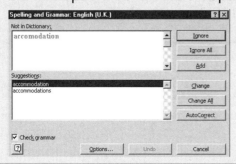

Figure 1.17 Spelling options

4   When you are sure you have chosen the correct word, click on <u>C</u>hange.
5   Once you have finished spellchecking your document, save as Exercise 1.14 and close the file. A correct version of this exercise can be found in the worked examples on the CD-ROM.

Capital letters

There are a few rules you need to know when using capital letters. If you are in any doubt then follow the draft given to you. The rules are as follows:

- Sentences should always start with a capital letter.
- A capital I should always be used if talking about yourself.
- Use a capital at the start of direct speech.
- Use initial capitals for names of people, places and proper nouns.
- Use capitals for days of the week and months of the year.
- Do not use capital letters for seasons.

Exercise 1.15

Key in the following text applying capital letters as appropriate. The correct version is given in the worked examples on the CD-ROM. Note how difficult it is to read without capital letters breaking up the sentences.

last sunday i went to visit my family in exeter, devon. it was a beautiful sunny day and there was a real feeling of spring in the air. we went to the local pub, the white horse for our lunch. the party comprised of my mother and father, my sister janet and my brother john. lunch was very good and afterwards we went for a stroll by the river exe. we left after having a cup of tea at a cafe called the teapot. it was agreed that we would spend another day together before long.

Setting tabs

You may need to set tab points so that you can line up work neatly. Look at Figures 1.18 and 1.19 below. This is a useful method of ensuring your work looks neat and tidy. For column work and tables it is suggested you use the table editor, information on which can be found on page 125.

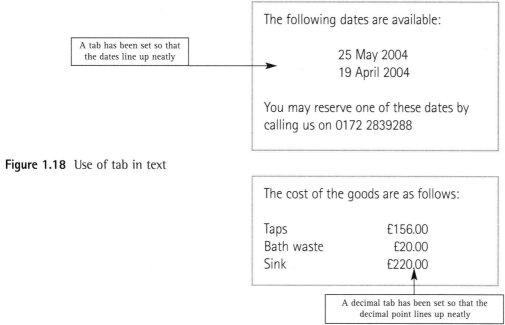

A tab has been set so that the dates line up neatly

The following dates are available:

25 May 2004
19 April 2004

You may reserve one of these dates by calling us on 0172 2839288

Figure 1.18 Use of tab in text

The cost of the goods are as follows:

Taps   £156.00
Bath waste   £20.00
Sink   £220.00

A decimal tab has been set so that the decimal point lines up neatly

Figure 1.19 Decimal tab

Left tabs align text to the left
          Centre tabs align to the centre of the tab point
                              Right tabs align text to the right
                    23.40

The various tabs were set at 6.5 cm

Figure 1.20 Alignment of tabs

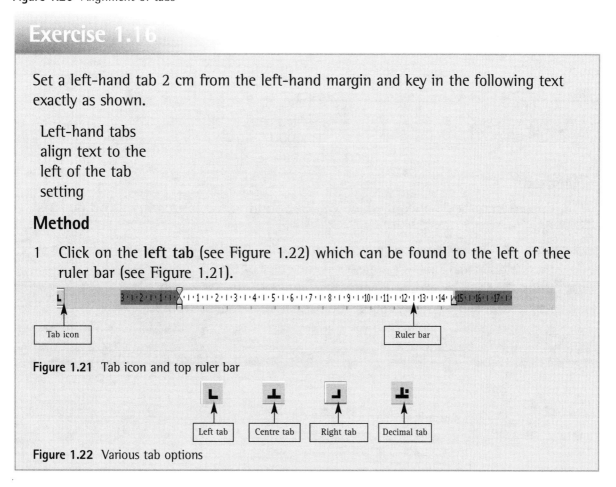

Exercise 1.16

Set a left-hand tab 2 cm from the left-hand margin and key in the following text exactly as shown.

Left-hand tabs
align text to the
left of the tab
setting

Method

1   Click on the **left tab** (see Figure 1.22) which can be found to the left of thee ruler bar (see Figure 1.21).

Tab icon

Ruler bar

Figure 1.21 Tab icon and top ruler bar

Left tab   Centre tab   Right tab   Decimal tab

Figure 1.22 Various tab options

2 Now click on the ruler bar at the 2 cm mark. A left tab icon will appear on the ruler bar.

3 Press the **tab** key on the keyboard to move to the tab point.

4 Key in the text and then press the **return** key. Repeat step 3.

Exercise 1.17

Set a right tab at 5 cm and key in the following text:

Right-hand tabs
align text to the right
of the tab setting

Method

1 Ensure that the **Tab** icon, which can be found in the left corner is on **right tab.**

2 Click on the **Right tab** icon and then click on the ruler bar at the 5 cm mark. A right tab will appear on the ruler bar.

3 Press the **tab** key on the keyboard to move to the tab point.

4 Key in the text and then press the **return** key. Repeat step 3.

Exercise 1.18

Set a decimal tab at 6.5 cm and key in the following text:

12.53
1920.66
1.20000
1,000,000.00

Method

1 Ensure that the **Tab** icon, which can be found in the left corner, is on **decimal tab.**

2 Click on the **Decimal tab** icon and then click on the ruler bar at the 6.5 cm mark. A decimal tab will appear on the ruler bar.

3 Press the **tab** key on the keyboard to move to the tab point.

4 Key in the text and then press the **return** key. Repeat step 3.

Exercise 1.19

Practise setting tabs by keying in the following tables:

Chocolate	Boiled Sweets	Toffees
Sherbet	Liquorice	Humbugs
Pear Drops	Mints	Wine gums

1.99	19.99	199.99
0.760	000.760	00000.76000
43.85	438.5	43800000.00

Accessing the Help function

In this section you will learn about:

- the Help function in Word
- Undo and Redo buttons

The Help function

At some point you may need to access the various Help options. To access the **Help** function, do the following:

Exercise 1.20

Access the **Help** function using various methods.

Method 1

1 Press the **F1** button at the top of the keyboard. The **Help** assistant will appear on screen. Key in a question relating to the help you require.

Method 2

1 Click on the **Help** button on the toolbar. [?] ▾

Method 3

1 Click on the <u>H</u>elp button on the menu bar.

Undo/Redo

If you have made a mistake and wish to go back to where you were, you can use the **Undo/Redo** buttons which are situated on the toolbar (see Figure 1.23).

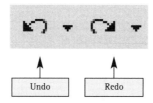

Figure 1.23 Undo and Redo buttons

The **Undo** button will remove the last action one by one to a maximum of 20. (The number of undo actions can be changed by choosing **Options** on the **Tools** menu. Go to the **Edit** tab).

The **Redo** button will redo an action that has been undone.

Formatting documents 2

In this section you will learn about:

- sub or shoulder headings
- text alignment

Use sub or shoulder headings

Sub or shoulder headings appear within the text to separate pieces of information or topics and make reading the article easier and clearer.
Look at Figure 1.24 below.

MAIN HEADING

<u>Sub Headings</u>

These are often underlined, however other types of emphasis can be used including bold with initial capitals, italic or any other combination.

<u>Sub Headings</u>

You must be consistent with the headings – they should be in the same style and font all the way through the document. The spacing before and after the headings must also be consistent.

Figure 1.24 Headings

You can see that there is a clear line space before and after the sub or shoulder headings and that emphasis has been used to clarify the heading. You must ensure that you are consistent with the display of sub or shoulder headings. Check the following very carefully:

- font
- font size
- capitalisation
- spacing before and after the heading.

Text alignment

The alignment of the text can also vary. Look at Figure 1.25 below.

This text is left aligned and has a ragged right-hand margin. This means that all the lines start at the left-hand margin. The right-hand margin is allowed to occur naturally. You should not press enter at the end of each line.

This text is centred.
This means that each line is centred between the margins.
The enter key has been pressed at the end of each line.

This text is right aligned. This means the text flows from the right-hand margin to the left. The enter key has not been pressed at the end of each line, so that the text will flow naturally. This type of text is normally only used for headings or when creating a piece of display work.

This text is justified. This means the text is aligned to both the left and right margins. The software will automatically add extra space to the text in order to ensure the lines end at the same place. It can be difficult to read large blocks of text that have been justified. The ragged edge helps guide the eye. This display is often used for reports.

Figure 1.25 Text alignment

Exercise 1.21

Key in the following text. Use single line spacing, and a justified right margin. Centre the heading. Correct any spelling or typographical errors you find.

Save the document as Exercise 1.21. A correct version of this exercise can be found in the worked examples on the CD-ROM.

PHOENIX GROUP PLC

WHO ARE WE?

Phoenix Group plc is a large public limited company with business interests in many areas. Founded in 1959 by Alex Cross and Sara Davies, it has grown into one of the country's largest and most popular limited companies.

WHAT DO WE DO?

Phoenix Group plc has many and varied business interests. From corporate hospitality, through retail and Internet shopping to travel agencies and holiday operators. We believe diversification is the key to a successful business.

HOW WELL DO WE DO IT?

Our market share is large and our stock price has shown consistent growth over the past five years. Our shareholders have enjoyed dividend increases during this period. Our profit forecast for this year shows a 16% increase. We feel justifiably proud of our achievements.

Method

1 Go to the text alignment tools on the **Toolbar**. If they are not available, you can add them to your toolbar by going to **View**, **Toolbars**, **Formatting**.

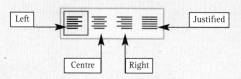

Figure 1.26 Text alignment icons

2 Click on the **Centre** icon and then key in the heading. Press the **return** key twice to leave a clear line space after the heading.
3 Click on the **Justified** icon so that the body of the text is fully justified.

Part 2

Text production

The Level 1 Text Production examination offered by OCR consists of three tasks:

1   A letter keyed in on headed paper
2   A memo keyed in using a memo form
3   A report or article

You may use either a typewriter or a word processor.

Throughout the three tasks there will be the following:

- Words that need to be corrected (these will be circled), including spelling errors, punctuation, apostrophes, omitted full stops and errors of agreement
- Abbreviations which need to be expanded
- Emphasis of text
- Amendments using correction signs
- Information to be transferred from one document to another
- Information which must be keyed in using a consistent format
- Use of double and single line spacing

You are allowed 1 hour and 15 minutes in which to complete the examination.

In this section you will learn about the following:

- Business letters
- Essential English – abbreviations
- Memos
- Consistency 2
- Essential English - apostrophes
- Essential English - errors of agreement
- Consolidation practice

- Consistency 1
- Correction signs
- Essential English – spelling
- Articles and reports
- Checking details to provide information
- Taking the examination

Business letters

In this section you will learn about:

- headed paper
- templates
- references
- inserting a date

- name and address block
- salutation
- paragraphs
- complimentary close
- enclosures

You will need to know how to set out a business letter correctly. Look at Figure 2.1 below.

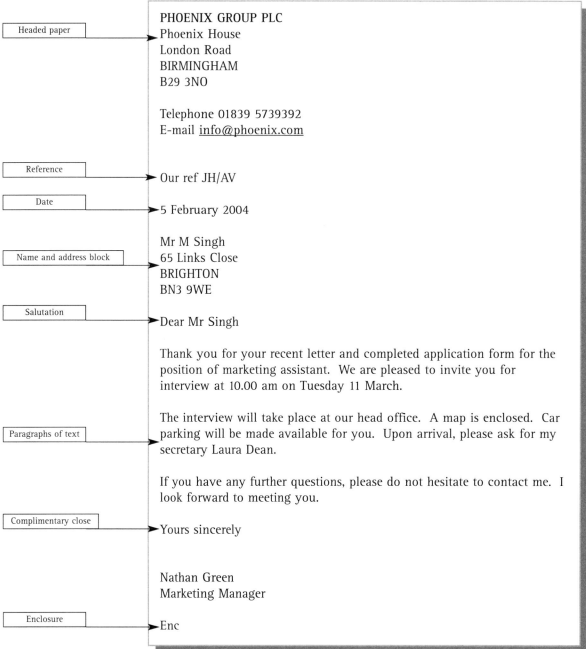

Headed paper

PHOENIX GROUP PLC
Phoenix House
London Road
BIRMINGHAM
B29 3NO

Telephone 01839 5739392
E-mail info@phoenix.com

Reference

Our ref JH/AV

Date

5 February 2004

Name and address block

Mr M Singh
65 Links Close
BRIGHTON
BN3 9WE

Salutation

Dear Mr Singh

Thank you for your recent letter and completed application form for the position of marketing assistant. We are pleased to invite you for interview at 10.00 am on Tuesday 11 March.

Paragraphs of text

The interview will take place at our head office. A map is enclosed. Car parking will be made available for you. Upon arrival, please ask for my secretary Laura Dean.

If you have any further questions, please do not hesitate to contact me. I look forward to meeting you.

Complimentary close

Yours sincerely

Nathan Green
Marketing Manager

Enclosure

Enc

Figure 2.1 Business letter

This letter has been displayed in a **blocked** style – that means all the lines start at the left-hand margin. The punctuation is **open punctuation** – that is, the standard items such as name and address block, salutation, heading and complimentary close do not contain punctuation. The main text does, of course, contain punctuation.

Headed paper

Business letters should always be presented on headed paper. This may be provided as pre-printed paper that you feed into the computer printer, or may be a template saved on the computer.

Pre-printed paper is more common in the workplace. If you use this you will need to do the following:

- Set the top margin of the page to allow for the heading at the top of the paper. To do this, you will need to measure the amount of space taken up with the pre-printed heading. Now alter the top margin of using the page setup method (see page 7) by that amount.
- Work out how the paper is loaded into your printer. This varies from printer to printer and so you will need to ask your tutor.

Alternatively, you may use a template that has been loaded onto your computer. If this is the case, you will need to do the following:

- You will need to know the name of the template. Each time you key in a letter you will need to open that file.
- Once you have used the template to key in the letter, you must ensure that you save the document using a different name. If you do not and just save the letter after keying in then the new text will be saved onto the template.

There is a letter template provided on the CD-ROM that accompanies this book.

Exercise 2.1

Open the letter template called Headed Paper Template on your CD-ROM.

Method

1 Ensure the CD-ROM is inserted into the drive.
2 Go to **File** and choose **Open**. The following sub-menu will appear (Figure 2.2).

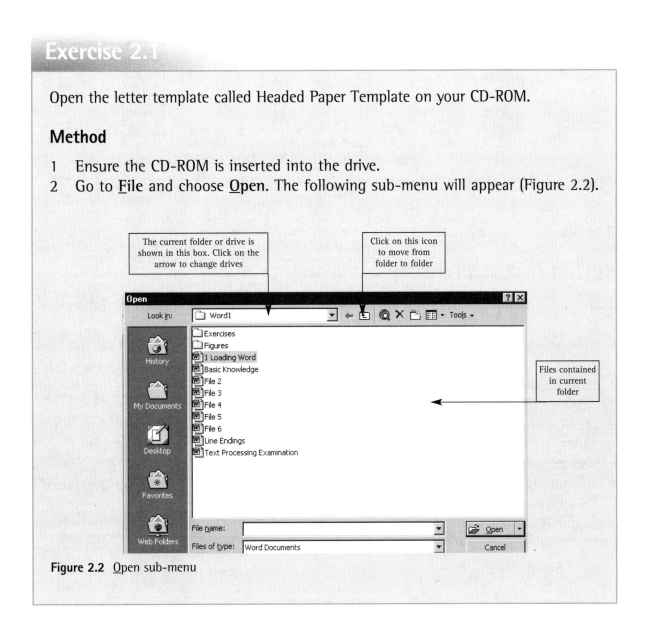

Figure 2.2 Open sub-menu

3   Click on the arrow next to the **Look in** box to see a list of drives and folders.
4   Click on the CD drive (the name of this may vary from PC to PC). The folders and files contained on the CD should appear.
5   Click on the folder called **Recall Documents**.
6   Click on the template called Headed Paper Template.
7   Click **Open**.

The template should now be on screen (see Figure 2.3).

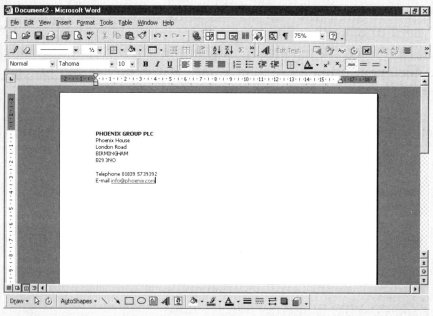

Figure 2.3 Headed paper template

Keying in a reference

You will be asked to key in a reference. Generally the rules for this are as follows:

*   The reference should be placed one clear line space after the heading on the paper (if you are using a template). If you are using pre-printed paper then it will be the first item you key in.
*   You should always follow the draft to ensure the capitalisation is correct.
*   Follow the draft to see if you should key in 'Our Ref' or 'Our Reference' in full.
*   There must be at least one clear space between the words 'Our Ref' and the actual reference.
*   If you are using open punctuation, do not type a full stop if the word 'reference' is abbreviated.

Exercise 2.2

Using the template you opened in Exercise 2.1, you will now key in the reference 'Our ref HF/MJ'.

Method

1 Click at the bottom of the headed paper as shown in Figure 2.3.
2 Press the **return** key twice to ensure that there is at least one clear line space between the headed paper and the reference.
3 Key in the reference exactly as shown, starting at the left-hand margin.

Date

All letters must have a date. The exam paper will not tell you to insert the date – you will be expected to remember this. It is important that you do insert the date – if you forget you will lose 3 marks. The rules are as follows:

- Leave a clear line space between the reference and the date (press **Enter** twice).
- Key in the date in full, eg 25 June 2004.
- If using open punctuation, do not type in 'th', 'rd' etc. and do not use commas to separate the month and the year.

You may use the automatic **date and time** insertion available on Word. To use this, do the following:

Exercise 2.3

Continue using the letter template from Exercise 2.1. Insert today's date in the correct position (see Figure 2.1).

Method

1 Ensure that there is a clear line space between the reference and the date insertion point.
2 Go to **Insert** on the toolbar and choose **Date and Time**. The following sub-menu will appear (Figure 2.4).

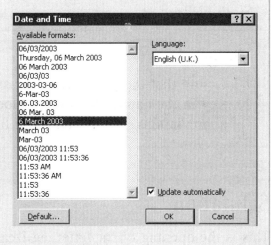

Figure 2.4 Insert date and time menu

2   Check that the <u>L</u>anguage box on the right-hand side of the dialogue box is set to English (UK).

3   Choose a format from the <u>A</u>vailable Formats box on the left-hand side, by clicking on the style of date you wish to use. Remember that the date must be in date, month, year order. If you use an American style (ie month, date, year order) you will be penalised in an examination. The best choice for examination purposes is date, month in full, year in full, eg 20 March 2004.

4   Click OK.

Name and address block

It is very important to key this in accurately otherwise the letter might not reach its destination! To key in the name and address block do the following:

- Key in the block after the date or special mark if there is one, leaving a clear line space.
- If you are using open punctuation, do not type a full stop after any capitals or insert a comma at the end of each line.
- The town must be keyed in in CAPITALS.
- Key in any abbreviations, such as Rd, Ave, Grdns. etc in full.
- County names may be kept as abbreviations.
- Always use a separate line for the postcode. This should be displayed in two separate blocks, eg BA1(space)8QP.

Exercise 2.4

Using the template you opened in Exercise 2.1, key in the following name and address:

Mrs H Finlay
28 Shelley Road
WINCHESTER
SO35 6NP

Method

1   Ensure that there is a clear line space after the special mark.

2   Key in the name and address block, remembering to expand any abbreviations. Ensure that each line of text starts at the left-hand margin.

Salutation

This is the opening of the letter, eg Dear Mr Stevens. Remember the following:

- Key in the salutation after the name and address block, leaving one clear line space.
- Do not use the person's initials in the salutation.
- Remember to use initial capitals.
- If using open punctuation, do not add a comma to the end of the line of text.

Exercise 2.5

Using the template you opened in Exercise 2.1, key in 'Dear Mrs Finlay' in the appropriate place.

Method

1 Ensure that there is a clear line space after the name and address block.
2 Key in 'Dear Mrs Finlay' at the left-hand margin, using the capitalisation as shown. Do not enter the initial (H) in the salutation. If you are using open punctuation, do not add a comma at the end of the salutation.

Paragraphs of text

These form the main body of the letter. The rules are as follows:

- Leave a clear line space between the salutation and the paragraphs of text.
- Leave a clear line space between each paragraph.
- Ensure that all paragraphs start at the left-hand margin. Unless specified, you should use a ragged right-hand margin for business letters.
- Do not forget to use punctuation in the text, even if you are using open punctuation.

Exercise 2.6

Using the template you opened in Exercise 2.1, key in the following paragraphs of text.

According to our records your car insurance policy will expire on the 2 April. We are sure you will wish to renew your insurance policy with us. We are pleased to tell you that our premiums have increased by only 0.5% this year. As a loyal customer you will also receive a 2.5% discount.

A renewal form is enclosed. Please complete, sign and return this as soon as possible. This will ensure your insurance cover is extended from the expiry date.

If you would like to discuss this matter further, please do not hesitate to contact me.

> **Method**
>
> 1   Ensure there is a clear line space between the salutation and the start of the text.
> 2   Key in the text, allowing it to wrap at the end of the line. This means you do not need to press return at the end of each line.
> 3   Ensure there is a clear line space between each paragraph of text.

Complimentary close

The complimentary close consists of 'Yours sincerely' or 'Yours faithfully', followed by a space large enough to put a handwritten signature. The name of the person who drafted the letter follows, often accompanied by their job title.

- Leave a clear line space after the paragraphs of text.
- The first word of the complimentary close should always have an initial capital.
- Remember, if you addressing the letter to a named person the close should be 'Yours sincerely'.
- If you are addressing the letter to 'Dear Sir' or 'Dear Madam' then you should use 'Yours faithfully'.
- Leave a minimum of 5 clear line spaces to ensure there is sufficient room for the signature.
- If asked to type the name of the person drafting the letter or the name of the company then follow draft for capitalisation.
- If keying in the name of the person, together with their job title, then put each on a separate line but do not leave a clear line space between.

Exercise 2.7

Using the template you opened in Exercise 2.1, key in 'Yours sincerely Martin Jacobs Renewals Manager' as a complimentary close.

Method

1   Ensure there is a clear line space between the end of the text and the start of the complimentary close.
2   Key in 'Yours sincerely', following the capitalisation as shown.
3   Press the **return** key 6 times in order to leave 5 clear line spaces.
4   Key in 'Martin Jacobs', press return.
5   Immediately under the name, key in Renewals Manager. Again, the capitalisation should be exactly as shown.

Enclosure(s)

If you are enclosing additional documents with a letter then you should indicate this at the bottom of the letter, after the complimentary close. You must check the draft of the document yourself to see if there are to be any enclosures as it will not be written on the examination paper.

As a general rule, you should do the following:

- Check the letter to see if it states 'we are enclosing' or 'attached is a ...'.
- Leave a clear line space after the complimentary close.
- Key in 'Enc', or if there is more than one enclosure 'Encs'.
- Do not key in a full stop after the abbreviation.

Exercise 2.8

Using the template you opened in Exercise 2.1, key in 'Enc' to indicate that there is an enclosure with the letter.

Method

1 Ensure you have a clear line space between the complimentary close and the start of the enclosure indicator.
2 Key in 'Enc' exactly as shown at the left-hand margin.

You have now completed the business letter. Save as Exercise 2.8 and print one copy. A correct version of this document can be found in the worked examples on the CD-ROM.

Exercise 2.9

Key in the following letter using the methods given above. Check your work carefully, amend any errors and print one copy. A correct version of this document can be found in the worked examples on the CD-ROM.

Our ref PJ/XY

Mr Percy Jackson
42 Lakeland Street
HULL
HU3 9KS

Dear Mr Jackson

Further to our meeting last week, we are pleased to enclose our quotation for the building works we discussed. We hope you will find it acceptable.

We believe our prices are very competitive. Please note that they include VAT. We have quoted on a fixed price basis. This means that the price will not increase for any reason.

As mentioned at our meeting, before this project can go ahead you will need to ensure that you do not need planning permission. The local authority will be able to advise you on this matter.

If you have any further questions please do not hesitate to contact us.

Yours sincerely

Xavier Young
Manager

Consistency 1

In this section you will learn about:

- punctuation
- words and figures
- money

You must ensure that when you are keying in text that you do so in a consistent style. This means that the formatting of the text, ie the font, font size etc., is the same throughout the document. This gives your work a neat, tidy and professional appearance.

Punctuation

You may use either open or full punctuation, however you must keep to the same style throughout. Do not mix the two or you will be penalised in an examination. It does not matter whether you leave one or two spaces after a full stop, but, again, whichever style you choose, keep to it throughout a document.

Words and figures

You may use either words or figures for keying in numbers in documents, but not both. It doesn't matter which you choose, but there are one or two exceptions:

- never start a sentence with a figure;
- never use the figure 1 when it is not referring to a measurement. For example, in the following sentence 'It is annoying when one is late for an appointment', it would be inappropriate to use the figure 1 in this instance.

Money

The rule for numbers also applies to sums of money. Once you have chosen a style you should keep to it, however you should quickly read through the document to see if there are any other numbers to be keyed in. For example, if you keyed in one pound (£1) in words but later found you had to key in sixty five thousand, seven hundred and forty two pounds (£65,742) then it would look better in figures.

You must also display sums of money consistently with regard to decimal places. For example, £10.00 and £5270.00 are both displayed with two decimal places.

If you are keying sums of money in columns then the decimal point must always be lined up and therefore hundreds, tens and units are also directly underneath each other. This will involve using the decimal tab, instructions on which can be found on page 18.

In the examination you should always display numbers, figures and sums of money as shown on the examination paper. This will ensure you do not lose any marks.

Exercise 2.10

Key in the following letter using the template Headed Paper. Using the rules shown above, use a consistent display for your work. Save as Exercise 2.10 and print one copy. A correct version of this document can be found in the worked examples on the CD-ROM.

Our ref LJ/2165

Mrs Laverne Dodds
48 Valletort Drive
PLYMOUTH
PL6 7XH

Dear Mrs Dodds

Thank you for your mortgage application received yesterday. After consideration Phoenix Financial are pleased to be able to offer you a mortgage of £125,000 for the purchase of the property 2 Swithin's Gardens, Plymouth. This offer assumes a purchase price of two hundred and sixteen thousand pounds.

Your mortgage will be fixed at 4.8% for three years. This is a discount of one per cent of our usual lending rate. The repayments for the loan over a twenty year period will be £285 per month.

A copy of our terms and conditions, together with two copies of our formal offer is enclosed. Please sign and return the formal offer if you wish to take up the loan.

Yours sincerely

Eric Ricco
Mortgage Manager

Essential English – abbreviations

When people are drafting documents, they often use abbreviations. It will be part of your work to know when to expand these abbreviations and to do so correctly.

At Level 1 you will need to know the following abbreviations and be able to expand them correctly.

Abbreviation	Expansion	Abbreviation	Expansion
a/c(s)	account(s)	org	organisation
approx	approximate(ly)	poss	possible
cat(s)	catalogue(s)	ref(s)	reference(s)
co(s)	company(ies)	ref(d)	refer(red)
dr	dear	sec(s)	secretary(ies)
info	information	sig(s)	signature(s)
opp(s)	opportunity/ies	temp	temporary
misc	miscellaneous	yr(s)	year(s)
		yr(s)	your(s)

There are also more common abbreviations that you should know:

Days of the week, eg Mon, Sat
Months of the year, eg Aug, Sept

Others include:

Complimentary closes

Abbreviation	Expansion
ffly	faithfully
sncly	sincerely

Words used in Addresses

Abbreviation	Expansion	Abbreviation	Expansion
road	road	sq	square
st	street	cres	crescent
ave	avenue	pl	place
dr	drive	pk	park

Exceptions

There are some words that will appear in an abbreviated format that you should not expand: NB, PS, plc, Ltd and the & when used in company names only. You should not expand 'Our Ref' or 'Your Ref' when it appears in a letter or memo heading.

Exercise 2.11

Key in the following letter, expanding the abbreviations where necessary. Save as Exercise 2.11 and print one copy. A correct version of this document appears in the worked examples on the CD-ROM.

Our ref TB/SG

Mr Terry Green
21 Hansford Sq
YORK
YO6 4NC

Dr Sir

With ref to yr recent enquiry, we are pleased to inform you that we have now received in stock the goods you ordered from our June cat. These will be despatched to you by recorded post.   A sign will be required upon delivery.

We apologise for the delay in sending these items. It appears that the manufacturers of the goods have been experiencing temp supply problems.

Yr a/c will be debited of the sum of £281 in approx 10 days' time. If you would like any further info regarding this order, please do not hesitate to contact us.

Yrs ffly

Gerald Pike
Manager

Correction signs

These are used in the workplace to show where errors and omissions must be amended. These may also be called proof marks or typescript signs and there are many of them. For the Text Processing examination you will only be expected to learn a few. You must ensure that you understand what is meant by each of them and that you learn these thoroughly.

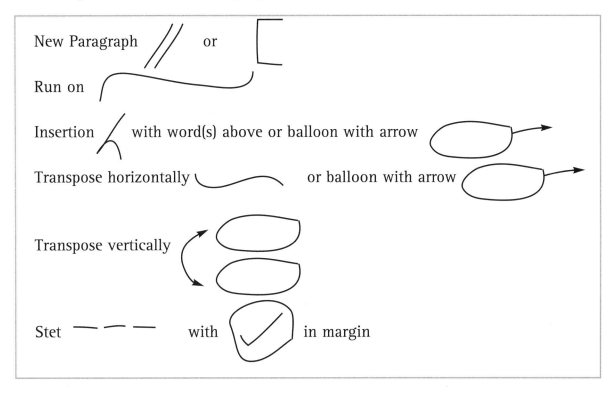

New paragraph

This means you should start a new paragraph. Remember to leave a clear line space between the two paragraphs.

Run on

This sign means you should join two paragraphs together, making one larger one. It is important that you remember to leave the correct number of spaces after the full stop of the first paragraph.

Insertion

You will need to insert the word or words exactly where the insertion sign appears. The words to be inserted are either written above the existing text or in a balloon that is situated elsewhere on the page. Check your work very carefully to ensure that you have inserted the text in the correct place.

Transpose horizontally or vertically

This means you need to move the text to a different location. For example, if you were asked to move the text horizontally then the sentence might look like this:

The basket of fruit contained, (pears, apples,) bananas, oranges and a pineapple.

The sentence should, after you have made the alteration, look like this:

The basket of fruit contained apples, pears, bananas, oranges and a pineapple.

If you are asked to move text vertically then you should swap the paragraphs so that they appear in different places. The most important thing to check is that you have moved all of the text requested.

Stet

This means to use the original word. You will see this sign where the editor has crossed out a word and then replaced it with a different word. The second word has also been crossed out. The editor will then put a row of dashes under the word that is to be used in the text. For example

The dog has a glossy ~~black~~ coat. *brown*

In this sentence the correct word is black.

Deletions

You may find that some words have been crossed out on the examination paper. You should not key in these words. However, sometimes there will be new words handwritten above the crossed out text. These new words will need to be keyed in. It is important to check you only miss out the words that have been crossed out – no more or less. The punctuation is also important. If, for example, you were told not to key in the last three words of a sentence, you should check whether the full stop has also been deleted on the exam paper. Don't forget, all sentences must have a full stop at the end.

Exercise 2.12

Key in the following letter, making corrections as indicated. Save as Exercise 2.12 and print one copy. A correct version of this exercise can be found in the worked examples on the CD-ROM.

Our ref MC/2169

Mr Stephen Kean
Kean + Co Ltd
42 Egerton Pk
HORNCHURCH
Essex
RM11 2AN

Dr Mr Kean

Further to our recent meeting I am pleased to tell you that the board of directors have approved yr plans for our new ~~luxury~~ offices.

The formal contract will be issued in the next ~~week~~ day or [N] so. In the meantime we will require clarification of a few points. This info will help us draw up the contract. We will contact you shortly regarding these.

We would like to stress that the contract will require you to guarantee the work will be completed on time. Failure to do so will result in financial penalty.

As you are aware, we will be setting up a temp office in a little used part of the building. We will need to have approx 100 square metres of space. This must be incorporated into yr schedule.

If you would like to discuss the contract, please do not hesitate to contact me.

Yrs sncly

Martin Crossley
Premises Manager

Exercise 2.13

Key in the following letter, making corrections as indicated. Save as Exercise 2.13 and print one copy. A correct version of this exercise can be found in the worked examples on the CD-ROM.

Our ref CL/SG

Mrs Cressida Langham
32 Perry Mead Ave
Acton
London
W3 6NO

Dr Mrs Langham

We have received today yr cheque for £500 sent in response to our appeal. We would like to take this opp to tell you how grateful we are for such a generous donation. This sum of money will help us to build a new shelter for the dogs and cats at our home. During the past yr or so, we have found that there are many more animals that require our assistance. We hope that our new shelter will provide additional accommodation for approx 50 dogs and 30 cats.

Yr donation will certainly help us to achieve this goal.

An info booklet is enclosed which we hope you will find interesting. If you would like any further info on the Centre please do not hesitate to contact us.

Yrs sncly
Sarah Greenslade
Director

Exercise 2.14

Key in the following letter, making corrections as indicated. Save as Exercise 2.14 and print one copy. A correct version of this exercise can be found in the worked examples on the CD-ROM.

Our ref GH/MJ
Mr Marcus Jamieson
49 Boston Rd
CROMER
Norfolk
NR29 4MO

Dr Mr Jamieson

Thank you for returning yr completed application form for the Assistant Design vacany.

I am pleased to tell you that you have been short-listed for this position and would like to invite you to interview. The interview will take place at 10.00am on 10 Feb. If this is not convenient, please contact my sec Daisy Young on extension 2039.

The interviewing panel will consist of myself, Harry Romaro, our design manager and Carys Miller, Senior design assistant. We would like to see a portfolio of yr recent work. Please bring approx 8-10 pieces with you.

A map giving directions to our offices is enclosed. On arrival at reception please ask for Daisy who will escort you to my office.
We look forward to meeting you.
Yrs sncly
Gary Helford
Director

Memos

In this section you will learn about:

- memo layouts
- references
- dating memos
- enclosures

A memo, or memorandum as it is sometimes called, is a document used to send messages to colleagues within an organisation. It is never used to send to customers outside of the company.

As with letters, you may use either a pre-printed memo form or a template stored on the computer. The layout of the memo form may vary from company to company, but should always contain the following:

- To – where the name of the person receiving the memo is keyed in.
- From – where the name of the person sending the memo is keyed in.
- Ref – the reference of the person sending the memo is keyed in here.
- Date – all business documents should contain a date.

A typical memo layout will look like Figure 2.5.

Memorandum

To

From

Ref

Date

Paragraphs of text to follow on from here

Figure 2.5 Typical memo form

When practising the exercises given in this book, use the MEMO template that is stored on the CD-ROM.

Exercise 2.15

Open the document called MEMO stored on the CD and key in the details as shown.

Method

1   You can, if you wish, line the cursor up with the 'o' in 'To' and then press the space bar twice in order to leave a clear space.
2   Now key in the words Paramitjit Kaur. However, this gives a rather untidy appearance and it is strongly recommended that you use the tab method shown on page 18. Figure 2.6 shows the appearance of the text using the tab method.

To	Paramitjit Kaur
From	Ursula Greenslade
Ref	PK/UG
Date	24 March 2002

Figure 2.6 Memo heading

You can see that each line starts in the same place, giving a uniform appearance, and that there is a small clear space between the longest line of the template (From) and the start of the name (Ursula Greenslade).
3   Now key in Ursula Greenslade lined up with the **From** line.

Reference

It is usual to give a reference in the memorandum. When you are keying in a reference, particularly for examination purposes, it is important that you follow the draft carefully to ensure that capitalisation is correct. You should use capital letters only where they are shown in the draft. The parts of the reference are separated using a forward slash / or oblique as it is called. Do not use a backward slash \ or you will lose marks.

You should not add your own initials to the reference given in the examination.

Exercise 2.16

Using the template you opened in Exercise 2.15, key in the reference 'PK/UG'.

Date

There must be a date on the memorandum. If a date is not given in the examination paper then you must insert the current date. For information on how to insert a date into your document see page 27.

Exercise 2.17

Using the template you opened in Exercise 2.15, insert today's date in the appropriate place.

Exercise 2.18

Using the template you opened in Exercise 2.15, key in the main text of the memo as shown below.

> I would be grateful if you could let your team know that the staff car park will be unavailable for the week commencing 23 August. This is because we are having the exterior of the building repaired and decorated during this period. There will be scaffolding and other building equipment in the area. The health and safety officer felt it would be much safer to close the car park for the week.
>
> Unfortunately, this will inconvenience a great many of the staff. The nearest car park is on Bolton Street, which is a few minutes walk from the office. It will not be possible for the company to reimburse staff's parking fees or offer any form of compensation.
>
> It is hoped that the car park will re-open on the 1 September. If the dates change then I will let you know immediately. A notice giving full details of these changes is attached. Please display this on the staff noticeboard.

Enclosure(s)

As with business letters, if you are enclosing additional documents with a memo then the enclosure(s) must be indicated. You must check the draft of the document to see if there are to be any enclosures yourself as it will not be written on the examination paper.

As a general rule, you should do the following:

- Check the memo to see if it states 'we are enclosing' or 'attached is a ...'.
- Leave a clear line space after the last line of text.
- Key in 'Enc', or if there is more than one enclosure 'Encs'.
- Do not key in a full stop after the abbreviation.

Exercise 2.19

Using the template you opened in Exercise 2.15, key in the enclosure indicator at the end of the text. Remember to leave a clear line space between the text and the enclosure indicator.

You have now completed the memo. Save as Exercise 2.19 and print one copy. A correct version of this exercise is shown in the worked examples on the CD-ROM.

Exercise 2.20

Using the MEMO template, key in the following document. Save as Exercise 2.20 and print one copy. A correct version is in the worked examples on the CD-ROM.

Memo

From   Grace Numan

To   Evan Kelston

Ref   GN/EK

Please find attached a letter from a Mr Henry Unwin. He recently purchased a patio heater from us and is very unhappy with the item. It appears there is a fault with the product and it does not give out any heat. When Mr Unwin returned the item to our Cardiff branch the staff were very unhelpful and refused to take the item back. As you can imagine, Mr Unwin is extremely upset at the way he has been treated.

I would be grateful if you could investigate this complaint. Mr Unwin should immediately be sent a letter of apology and a gift voucher for £25. Please speak to the staff at the Cardiff branch and find out why the customer was refused a refund. The manager must be told that he is responsible for ensuring staff are trained properly to handle complaints.

Please report back to me within the next few days, outlining the problems at the branch and suggesting some solutions.

Essential English – spelling

The examination requires you to be able to spell correctly words taken from the list below. You will also be expected to know and be able to spell their derivatives. These are the different endings of the same word, for example 'Accommodate' has the following derivatives: accommodated, accommodating, accommodative, accommodator, accommodation.

In order to select the correct derivative, you must read the text very carefully. Read for meaning and then the required word should be obvious.

You will need to learn the following list:

Accommodate	**Acknowledge**	**Advertisement**	**Appreciate**
Accommodated	Acknowledged	Advertised	Appreciated
Accommodating	Acknowledging	Advertising	Appreciating
Accommodation		Advertiser	
Believe	**Business**	**Client**	**Colleague**
Believed	Businesses	Clients	Colleagues
Believing			
Believer			
Believable			
Committee	**Correspondence**	**Definite**	**Develop**
Committees		Definitely	Develops
			Developed
			Developing
Expense	**Experience**	**Financial**	**Foreign**
Expenses	Experienced	Financially	Foreigner
	Experiencing		
Government	**Inconvenient**	**Receipt**	**Receive**
Governments	Inconveniently	Receipts	Receiving
Governmental	Inconvenience		Received
	Inconveniencing		
	Inconvenienced		
Recommend	**Responsible**	**Separate**	**Sufficient**
Recommendation	Responsibly	Separated	Sufficiently
Recommends		Separates	
		Separating	
		Separately	
Temporary	**Through**		
Temporarily			

Exercise 2.21

Key in the following memo, correcting any spellings that are incorrect. Save as Exercise 2.21 and print one copy. A correct version can be found in the worked examples on the CD-ROM.

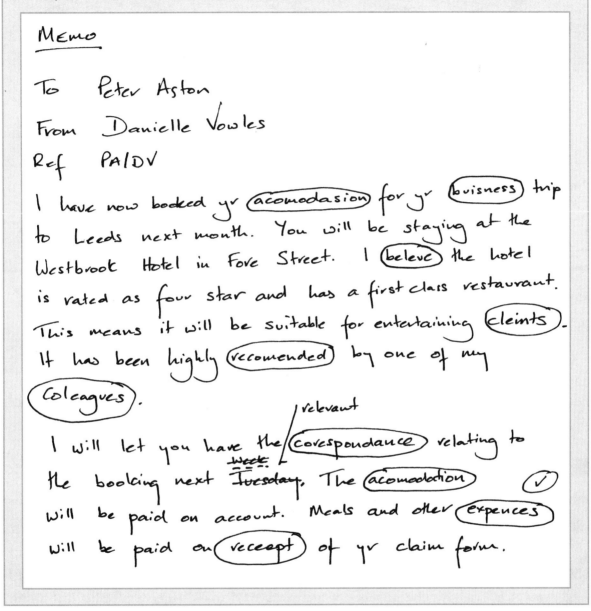

MEMO

To   Peter Aston

From   Danielle Vowles

Ref   PA/DV

I have now booked yr acomodasion for yr buisness trip to Leeds next month. You will be staying at the Westbrook Hotel in Fore Street. I beleve the hotel is rated as four star and has a first class restaurant. This means it will be suitable for entertaining cleints. It has been highly recomended by one of my coleagues.

I will let you have the/correspondance relevant relating to the booking next ~~Tuesday~~ week. The acomodation ✓ will be paid on account. Meals and other expences will be paid on receept of yr claim form.

Key in the following memo, making amendments as shown. Save as Exercise 2.22 and print one copy. A correct version can be found in the worked examples on the CD-ROM.

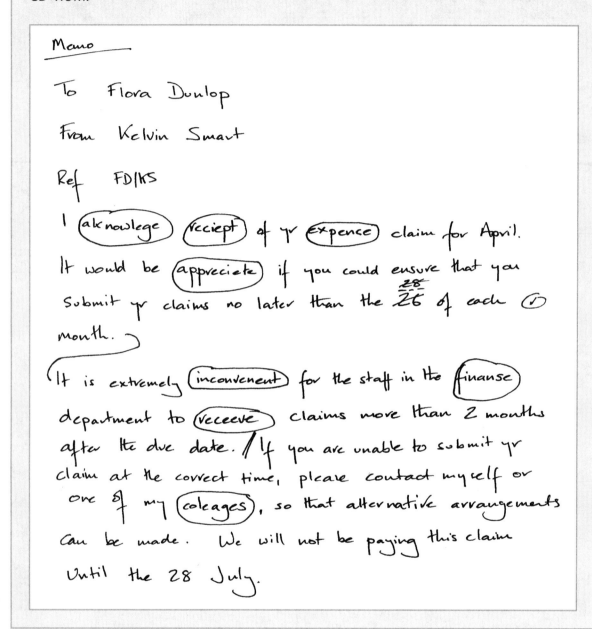

Consistency 2

In this section you will learn about:

- measurement and weights
- time
- percentages

Measurements/Weights

You can display these in words or figures as long as you keep to the same style. It is worth remembering that it is often easier to read figures as long measurements can become confusing in words. Look at the following example:

Twenty two centimetres multiplied by one metre seven centimetres OR
0.22 cm × 1.7 m

It is best to leave a space after the number and before the measurement. For example, 165 mm, 27 ltrs, 121 kg. Use the lower case letter x instead of the word multiply or times.

Time

You should always follow the draft given in the examination paper to see whether you are going to use the 12 or 24 hour clock. For the 12 hour clock, you will also need to be consistent in the display of hours and minutes.

Therefore, if you are going to be keying in both hours and hours and minutes the display should have a point (full stop) followed by the two minute figures (or zeros in the case of a full hour). If you are going to key in just hours then you do not need to key in the two zeros, the hour on its own will be sufficient. There should always be a space between the figures and the am/pm indicator. Look at the following examples:

5 pm, 8.30 am, 12 noon, 4.21 pm

For the 24 hour clock you must remember to key in the abbreviated form of hours (hrs) after the figures. There is no point in the 24 hour clock. It is usual to place a zero at the front of single figure times so that the display remains consistent. Look at the following examples:

1500 hrs, 2400 hrs, 0130 hrs, 0620 hrs

Percentages

If you are required to key in percentages you should always follow the draft on the examination paper. In the workplace, you could use any of the following styles:

25%   twenty-five per cent   25 per cent

Remember that if you are keying in other numbers in the same document, then you should use the same style for any percentages.

Exercise 2.23

Key in the following memo, making amendments as shown. Save as Exercise 2.23 and print one copy. A correct version appears in the worked examples on the CD-ROM.

Memo

To   Max Preston

From   Francesca Barrett

Ref   MP/FB

I have researched the train times for our trip to Exeter next week. In order to reach Exeter by 10.00 am we will need to catch the nine fifteen am from Paignton. The train will stop at Exeter Central which is the most convenient station for us.

It is scheduled to arrive at nine fifty five am. If you would prefer to get an earlier train then we should catch the 0857 hrs. This will arrive at 9.42 allowing us appox twenty minutes to reach the client's premises. As we are not too sure when we will be leaving I have researched journey times from 2.00 pm onwards. Trains leave Exeter Central at 1420 hrs and 1450 hrs and then every half hour until 5 pm. The journey is of approx 45 minutes' duration.

Please let me know which train you wish to catch.

Exercise 2.24

Key in the following memo, making amendments as shown. Save as Exercise 2.24 and print one copy. A correct version appears in the worked examples on the CD-ROM.

From   Daniel Robson

To   Francine Carllew

Ref   DR/FC

I attach a copy of a letter (received) from Jasmine Patel. You may remember I visited her offices last week to discuss the refurbishment of her new shop premises.

You will see from the letter that Jasmine is very interested in our services. Her only real concern is the time scale we discussed. Unfortunately, we are very busy during March. I am not sure we would be able to keep to the deadline she requires. This was fully explained at our meeting and Jasmine did express some concern at the time. I (bileive) Jasmine could become a very good customer of ours. She plans to open several new shops during the next yr or so. She has expressed her intention to use the same co for the refurbishment on each occasion.

It occurs to me that we might be able to solve this problem by asking the workforce to work on the Lenington project during the last weekend in Feb. This will free up 2 days and if we were able to work an extra hour or so each day then we should be able to finish the project three days earlier than expected.

(If this is not (possable)) then perhaps we could employ some temp staff for a few days.

Please let me have yr comments as soon as possible. If you have any other ideas, I would be very pleased to consider them.

Exercise 2.25

Key in the following memo, making amendments as shown. Save as Exercise 2.25 and print one copy. A correct version appears in the worked examples on the CD-ROM.

From   Sandy Heyworth

To   Jemima Black

Ref   JB/SH

Thank you for yr memo dated 14 June. I have now booked the exhibition stand for the Worldwide Trade Fair next Feb. Once confirmation has been received I will forward it to you for the files. The trade fair is open from 2 Feb through to 6 Feb. As we will need to set up and clear away the exhibition stand We will need to arrive on 1 Feb and leave the day after the exhibition closes.

We now need to find suitable accomodation. I beleve that the local hotels become heavily booked during this event. Please book 5 single rooms and three double rooms, all with en-suite facilities. The hotel should be situated close to the exhibition centre. The budget for accommodasion is £95 per single room and £150 per double, per night. I would like to have the rooms booked and confirmed by the end of the week.

We must have a meeting to discuss the various tasks that need to be carried out in order to make the exhibition a success. Please contact me as soon as possible with some available dates. early next month

Articles and reports

You will also need to key in an article or report. This is straightforward copy typing, but you will need to incorporate various instructions and amendments which are placed throughout the draft.

As well as expanding abbreviations and correcting errors you will also need to be able to do the following:

- change line spacing from double to single or vice versa
- emphasise words or sentences.

Changing line spacing

You have already looked at setting line spacing on page 9. The method given below in Exercise 2.26 shows you how to change the line spacing within a document.

Exercise 2.26

Key in the following text using single line spacing. The second paragraph only should be keyed in double line spacing. Save as Exercise 2.26 and print one copy. A correct version is in the worked examples on the CD-ROM.

PIRATES ⟨Use single linespacing⟩

many

Pirates have been around for thousands of years. Sailors from all countries including the ancient Greeks and Romans have been troubled by pirates roaming the seas and stealing their precious cargoes. Pirates or corsairs as they are also known, threatened the trading routes of Ancient Greece and seized cargoes of grain and olive oil, fine cloth, treasure and exotic spices.

This paragraph only in double linespacing

During the 17 century governors of Caribbean islands, such as Jamaica, paid buccaneers, which is another name for pirates, to attack Spanish treasure ships and ports. Although these raids began with official backing, the buccaneers soon became out of control and operated purely for their own gain. They attacked any ships they thought carried cargo of value regardless of the country of origin. In this way they became true pirates.

The reason for the success of so many pirate attacks is that their ships usually carried far bigger ~~larger~~ crews than usual. This meant they could easily out number their victims. They also made adjustments to the ships so that they could carry more cannon than merchant ships. Their reputation as terrifyingly brutal men preceded them and this also contributed to their great success. ⊘

Famous Pirates

The most famous of all pirates is Blackbeard. He was always heavily armed with knives, cutlasses and pistols. He tried to make himself look fearsome in order to intimidate his victims. One of the ways he did this was to place pieces of twisted fuse in his wild and matted hair. He would set light to these during battles so that his face was surrounded with smoke.

Although it is hard to believe, there were two famous women pirates, Anne Bonny and Mary Read. They were both crew members of a pirate ship led by 'Calico Jack'. They took part in many battles and fought as well as any of the men.

They were eventually captured and put on trial. As both women were pregnant, they escaped being hung, which was the fate of most of their fellow crew members.

Method

1 Key in the first paragraph of text. After you have finished keying in press the **return** key twice **whilst still in single line spacing** to start the second paragraph.

2 Now click on the **Double Line Spacing** icon ═

3 Key in the text for the second paragraph. Press return just once – remember you are in double line spacing. Now click on the **Single Line Spacing** icon

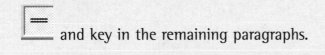 and key in the remaining paragraphs.

Note: If you use the above method the space between the paragraphs of text will be roughly equal. If you use any other method the space between the paragraphs will be unequal, thus giving an inconsistent appearance.

Emphasis

You may be asked to emphasise a word or sentence. The most usual form of emphasis is to embolden the text. Look at Figure 2.7, which gives examples of common forms of emphasis.

Embolden – This makes the characters darker and slightly thicker. It is the most common form of emphasis.

<u>Underscore</u> or <u>Underline</u> – Before computers this was the only form of emphasis. Nowadays it is not used as much as a main form of emphasis but is often used together with bold or italics.

Italic – The letters slope to the right. It is not the most suitable form of emphasis for headings as, unless you use italic and bold together, it does not stand out very well.

Figure 2.7 Common types of emphasis

You can, of course, use more than one type of emphasis at a time. For example, **Italic and Bold** work well together, as does *Italic and Underline*. <u>**Underline and Bold**</u> can also be used, but appears rather heavy on the page.

Exercise 2.27

Key in the following text, using emphasis where indicated. Save as Exercise 2.27 and print one copy. A correct version appears in the worked examples on the CD-ROM.

(handwritten note, circled) Use double linespacing

The Red Arrows

The RAF Aerobatic Team, the *Red Arrows* is recognised worldwide. Their daring displays of **precision flying** have been enjoyed by many hundreds of thousands of *(circled: peo5ple)* in countries all over the world.

Formation

(handwritten) The team was established in 1966 with a total crew of 9 pilots. However, 2 pilots were trained as reserves. This proved unsuccessful as each crew member has a highly individual and specialised role. The two reserves needed to be trained to fill each of the crew members' positions. This meant that although they were the most specialised of all the pilots, they only had reserve positions.

In 1968 the practice of training two reserve pilots was ~~stopped~~ *finished* and the display team was *(✓)* increased from 7 to 9 members. The classic **Diamond Nine** formation has come to represent the peak of precision flying and is the team's trademark. *(handwritten)* There is, however, a tenth member of the team. He flies a spare jet to each of the shows in case of a breakdown. This pilot never flies in public displays.

Length of Service

(handwritten: crew)
The amount of time spent with the *Red Arrows* is reasonably short. A ~~team~~ *crew* member usually *(✓)* spends three seasons with the team. The *Snychro Pair*, that is numbers 6 and 7 of the team, perform solo manoeuvres in the display.

These are very popular and add great excitement and interest to the show. The manager of the *Red Arrows* gives the commentary which accompanies the display.

(handwritten note, circled) This paragraph only in single linespacing

Method 1

1   Go to the emphasis icons that appear on the toolbar.

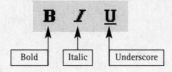

Figure 2.8 Emphasis icons

2   Choose the type of emphasis you wish to use, by clicking on the icon.
3   Key in the text you wish to emphasise.
4   Click on the icon again to switch off the emphasis.

Note: You can also use this method after you have keyed in the text. To do this key in the text, then highlight it. Now, click on the relevant icon and the text will be emphasised.

Method 2

1   Go to **Format** on the menu bar. Select **Font**, and the following sub-menu will appear.

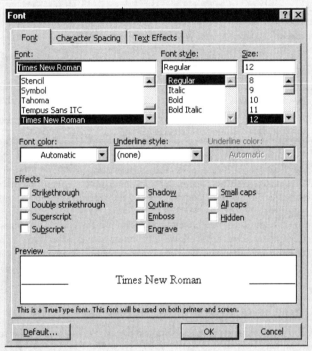

Figure 2.9 Font sub-menu

2   In the **Effects** menu check the appropriate box(es) and click **OK**.

Method 3

1   Hold down the **Ctrl** key and press the relevant emphasis shortcut key – B for **Bold, I** for Italic and U for Underscore.
2   Key in the text – the text will be automatically emphasised.
3   To switch off the emphasis, hold down the **Ctrl** key and press the relevant shortcut key.

Be very careful when emphasising text in the examination that you do not emphasise too much or too little as marks will be lost.

Exercise 2.28

Key in the following text, emphasising words as shown. Save as Exercise 2.28 and print one copy. A correct version appears in the worked examples on the CD-ROM.

Use double linespacing

PATCHWORK QUILTING

Emphasise this word

Quilting has been a favourite hobby for many hundreds of years. Practical and creative, there are examples of beautiful stitching and intricate designing going back many hundreds of years. Patchwork hasn't always been used for quilting. It was also for wall hangings and even sails for boats. It is an economical way of making quilts and was at the forefront of recycling as patchwork used the best pieces of old garments and sheets to make up the designs.

This paragraph only in single linespacing

The earliest quilts were thought to have been made of wool, however, one of the oldest surviving patchwork quilts was made of chintz. This hard-wearing and washable fabric was ideal for making quilts and other home furnishings. The art of patchwork involved making paper templates that were then put together to make the design. The pieces of fabric were cut to match the template and then stitched together following the straight lines. By using templates it is possable to design quite intricate quilts. One of the most common designs is the medallion which has a central design with applique around the edges.

In America, quilting became very fashionable and something of a social occupation. Quilting Bees were frequently held and these were very important social gatherings. Women would often travel a great distance to attend such an event. Best cloothes would be worn and it was considered extremely important to be invited to your neighbour's 'bee'. The quilting frames were set up and the hostess would provide scissors and thread. News and gossip were exchanged as the women stitched. Young women would spend time at these events learning to stitch and therefore prepare themselves for the housewifely duties they would need to perform once married.

The patterns of the quilts would take on special significance. Weddings, births and deaths were all represented by the various patterns. Quilts often became prized heirlooms passed from one generation to another. A fascinating record of family history.

Essential English – apostrophes

You are expected to ensure that apostrophes are used correctly in the examination. The rules for learning when to use an apostrophe are simple, but sometimes it can be difficult to see exactly where an apostrophe should be.

Keep in mind there are only two reasons for using an apostrophe – to show possession and to show omission of a letter or letters.

Showing possession

This is often the most difficult to decide. Basically, the apostrophe should be used when the item 'belongs' to something. For example, 'The dog's food bowl was empty'. Here the food bowl 'belongs' to the dog. Another example would be: 'the manager's diary'. You could turn this round and say 'the diary belonging to the manager'.

The only tricky decision to be made is when you are dealing with singular nouns or names that end in s. For example, if you wanted to say the bike belonging to James, where would the apostrophe be?

In this example, you would place the apostrophe at the end of James and then add an s: 'James's bike'. However, if applying this rule means that there will be a complicated sound, and a double or treble s, then add the apostrophe at the end of the word.

These rules are simple enough, but it does get more complicated when dealing with plurals. For example: 'The ladies' coats were stolen from the cloakroom'. Here the coats (plural) belong to the ladies (plural). The apostrophe should be placed at the end of the word 'ladies'.

When looking at possession remember the following:

- If there is only one owner (ie lady, cat, girl, man) then add an **apostrophe + s**, eg lady's, cat's, girl's, man's.
- If there is more than one owner (ie ladies, cats, girls) then just add the **apostrophe**, eg ladies', cats', girls'.

Some words, however, change completely when they move from singular to plural, eg child/children, man/men. Certain words change their endings, eg lady/ladies, company/companies. These will still need an apostrophe if they relate to possession. You should remember the following when dealing with plurals:

- If the plural does not end in 's' add an **apostrophe + s**, eg children's toys, men's overcoats.
- If the plural ends in s, then add the **apostrophe**, eg ladies' handbags, nurses' uniforms.

To show omission

An apostrophe can also be used to shorten certain words, eg don't, can't, wouldn't, you're. The rule for this is quite simple:

- When showing omission, place the apostrophe at the point where the letters are missing.

This is relatively straightforward, however there are two words that are often used incorrectly. These are its/it's and your/you're.

Its/It's

The way to test whether an apostrophe is needed is to see if you can substitute the words 'it is' instead of 'it's'. For example, if you said 'It's a lovely day' then it would also make sense to say 'It is a lovely day'. However, if you tried this example with 'The dog has finished its dinner', then it would not make sense ('The dog has finished it is dinner'), so an apostrophe is not needed.

- If you can substitute the words 'it is' then an apostrophe is required.

Your/You're

These two can cause trouble, however you need to think about these in the same way as its/it's. If you can substitute 'you are' in the sentence then an apostrophre is needed. For example: 'Your hair looks nice today'. If you were to substitute 'you are' then it wouldn't make any sense, 'You are hair looks nice today'. However, if you were to say 'You're the first to arrive', then you could substitute 'you are' for the sentence to make sense, 'You are the first to arrive'.

- If you can substitute the words 'you are' then an apostrophe is required.

Exercise 2.29

Key in the following article, making amendments as shown. Save as Exercise 2.29 and print one copy. A correct version appears in the worked examples on the CD-ROM.

Use double linespacing

CHIPMUNKS

Chipmunks are part of the rodent family, which in turn is the largest single order of mam9mals. They are gnawing animal's and possess a pair of chisel shaped incisors on each jaw. rodents do not have large canine teeth but have cheek teeth which they use for grinding their food. The common name for the chipmunk is ground squirrel. *Emphasise this sentence.*

This section only in single linespacing

Appearance

The Chipmunks' fur is short, and light to reddish brown in colour. It has 5 dark brown or black stripes running along its back. They are *It is* between 15-18 centimetres long and has a bushy tail that is about the same length as it's body.

Temperament

They are naturally friendly and inquisitive animals. If they are handled when young, they will become quite tame. This should be kept in mind when handling.

Feeding

You will need to provide a balanced diet for your pet. Give it a mixture of dry food, such as nuts and sunflower seeds and suppplement this with fresh apple or orange pieces. Fresh water must be availible in a plentiful supply.

Chipmunks are, however, very fast and agile.

Essential English – errors of agreement

An error of agreement is a grammatical error. For example, if you said 'We <u>is</u> going to the cinema later', then you have made an error of agreement as the subject and verb do not agree.

Look at the following sentence:

The dog are having its tea.

This is obviously incorrect. There is only one dog and therefore the sentence should read *The dog <u>is</u> having its tea.* If there were two or more dogs then the sentence should read *The dogs are having their tea.* This is a very easy example. It becomes more confusing with sentences such as the one below:

The party of tourists are late.

On the surface this may sound correct, but in fact it is wrong. The sentence is referring to only one party of tourists and so the verb is singular. The sentence should read *The party of tourists is late.*

One of the rules to remember is that company titles, and those of books and films etc., are singular because they refer to one item. Therefore, when you are writing use the singular verb. Look at the examples below:

McDonald's is a company that sells fast food.
The Rolling Stones is a group that was popular in the sixties.
Marks & Spencer is one of Britain's most popular shops.

However, if you were referring to more than one person then you would use the plural verb. Look at the examples below:

John and Kulvinder are planning a trip to Florence.
Dan and Ben were members of a band in the seventies.

There may well be an error of agreement in the examination paper for you to correct. It will be circled as an error and you must ensure that you amend it.

Exercise 2.30

Key in the following article, making amendments as shown. Save as Exercise 2.30 and print one copy. A correct version appears in the worked examples on the CD-ROM.

CRUISING HOLIDAYS

Many people now enjoy taking a holiday on a cruise liner. These holidays are not as ~~pricey~~ *expensive* as you might think as there are many (company's) now offering this type of trip.

There can be many advantages in taking a cruise as the liners cater for many different tastes. There will be a large number of activities on board that will suit all ages and interests.

Entertainment

Although there will be days during yr cruise when you are confined to the ship there (is) many different things to do. Most liners have gymnasiums, [theatres], [cinemas] and a swimming pool. to keep you entertained. Other activities offered include deck sports, lectures, demonstrations and cabaret shows.

(Accomodation)

There (are) usually a choice of accommodation on board to suit all pockets ~~from small to large~~. From basic two berth cabins to luxury suites, you will be able to find something that suits your price (range) All accommodation will have en-suite facilities.

Destinations

Cruise liners operate all over the world and you can choose from ~~various~~ *a wide range of* exotic locations. It is also (posseble) to take a two-part holiday. This means that you can spend a week or two on a cruise liner and then relax for the rest of your vacation at a seaside resort or similar. These *packages* offer the best of both worlds.

This section only in single linespacing

Exercise 2.31

Key in the following article, making amendments as shown. Save as Exercise 2.31 and print one copy. A correct version appears in the worked examples on the CD-ROM.

Use Double linespacing

Mythical Creatures ◄ *Emphasise this heading*

Myths and legends play a large part in history. Exciting stories of daring heroes, Greek and Roman Gods and mythical creatures have formed the basis of classical literature, operas, plays and many other forms of entertainment. There is a number of mythical creatures that feature in modern stories. Described below are just a few of the creatures you may have heard about.

The Unicorn

This magical animal is one of the most familiar of all mythical creatures. It has proved fascinating to many for thousands of years. The pure white animal looked rather like a horse or deer, but had a single straight horn growing out of its head.

This paragraph only in single linespacing

It were believed that the unicorns horn had magical healing powers. It was thought that if you made a cup from the horn and then drank from it you would be protected from various diseases and even poisoning.

Unicorns were thought to be difficult to catch as they were supposed to be very fast. Legend says that unicorns could only be caught by virtuous young women. However, if you attacked them they would fight back, stabbing you with it's sharp, pointed horn.

The Griffin

The griffin is reported to be around 5,000 years old. It were first seen in Ancient Egypt and takes the form of half lion and half eagle. Legend says that as both the king of animals and the king of birds makes this creature, it is the king of all mythical beasts.

It is said The legend states that Alexander the Great once captured four mighty griffins and chained them to a chariot.

As the griffins tried to fly away, they lifted the chariot into the air and Alexander took a trip over the land and sea. The Griffins flew so high that the sun burned their wings.

The Kraken

staring eyes and

This sea monster has large tentacles that can wreck a ship. It has terrified sailors for thousands of years.

Legend has it that the kraken floats on the surface of the water and gives the appearance of a small island to any passing sailors. As the ships got closer to the island, the kraken would pull the ship under the water and eat all the men on board. It is said that when the world must end, a monster will rise from the sea to kill anyone on the water.

It is thought that the giant squid may be the real-life kraken.

Exercise 2.32

Key in the following article, making amendments as shown. Save as Exercise 2.32 and print one copy. A correct version appears in the worked examples on the CD-ROM.

TEDDY BEARS

Teddy bears is one of our most loved toys. Young and old alike love the comfort that a teddy bear can bring. How did the teddy bear become a soft, cuddly toy when it real life it is a rather fierce and unfriendly wild animal?

Stieff

The teddy bear was first produced ~~as a soft toy in~~ around 1879 by a woman named Margarete Stieff. Margarete owned and ran a successful dressmaking business in Geingen in Southern Germany.

She found a pattern for a toy *elephant* in a magazine and made a few to sell to clien3ts. These were so successful she started to make other animals including bears.

Emphasise this sentence

Roosevelt

It is reputed that President Theodore Roosevelt, who was known as Teddy to his friends, gave the teddy bear its name. Apparently although the President was an avid bear hunter he refused to shoot a bear cub captured during a hunting expedition. A cartoonist, Clifford Berryman turned the incident into a cartoon. After that ~~point~~ all cartoons featuring President Roosevelt contained a picture of a bear. The bear then became known as Teddy's bear.

In 1892 Margarete decided to make bears a part of her business, selling them as children's toys. By the following year she had four employee's and ten outworkers' as the range had become so successful.

The range captured the imagination of the American people and by 1902 over one million teddy bears had been made by Steiff.

These was exported to many different countries. Steiff is still one of the leading manufacturer's of teddy bears today.

This section in single linespacing

Checking details to provide information

You may be asked to check details in one of the following ways:

- Transfer information from one task to another – eg a date, or a figure.
- Provide a date for a few weeks ahead – you may use a calendar for this task.
- Check the spelling of a word used in a previous task – eg a name or address.

This sounds easy enough, but you must be sure not to make any errors whilst transferring the information. Given below are some hints on how to ensure you can check details successfully.

- Read the instructions very carefully.
- Do not rush to find the information and pick the wrong material. Look carefully at the examination paper and check that you have chosen the correct information.
- Provide only the correct information – not too much nor too little.
- Copy the words exactly, paying particular attention to names, dates, times etc.
- Check that when you have entered the information the work makes sense. If it doesn't you may find that you have used the wrong information.

Consolidation practice

The following consolidation exercises will help you prepare for the Text Production examination. Try to complete each set of consolidation pieces in the usual time allowed for this examination, that is 1 hour and 15 minutes.

Remember to check your work carefully, and correct any errors before printing. You should print one copy of each document. Correct versions of these exercises can be found in the worked examples on the CD-ROM.

Consolidation practice 1 – Document 1

Our ref AD3210

Mrs B Newland
Morton Ltd
Hanley Business Park
READING
RG5 6BY

Dr Mrs Newland

Thank you for yr recent order. I can confirm that the (advertisemint) has now been booked. Yr series will run from next month's issue of LifeStyle Magazine for three months.

You will be sent a proof copy of the advertisement approx 2 weeks before publication date. Please ensure that you check this and return it within two days. If you need to make a correction at this point it can be made free of charge. Once the deadline for returning copy has passed we will make a charge for any further corrections.

All our (advertiseing) (cleints) will (recieve) a copy of LifeStyle Magazine so that they can view their advertisement. This will be sent one week after publication date. (free of charge)

Yr co will be invoiced at the end of each month. Payment can be made by credit or debit card, cheque or direct debit. Please ensure payment is made within ten days of (receiptt) of invoice. A copy of our terms and conditions of business is enclosed for yr info. ~~Further details will be provided on request~~

We wish you much success with yr campaign.

Yrs sncly

Hannah Box
Advertising Manager

Document 2

From   Hannah Box

To   Peter Westlake

Ref   AD/HB

This is the memorandum

Massive

We have had a ~~large~~ amount of enquiries for ✓ the classified advertsing section of the magazine during the past few days. A number of cleints have taken advantage of the discounted rates for series bookings. //I beleeve that we could increase the number of bookings if we offered a better financial incentive. I have undertaken some market research and ↓ other publications offer a free insertion if clients book more than four advertisements.

it would appear that

It would also appear that the amount of time between clients booking an advertisement to publication is to long. Other magazines allow bookings up to two weeks before printing. We are currently insisting upon four weeks. Proof copies go out two w— before printing. I would be grateful if you could look at reducing this time.

Please let me have yr thoughts within the next week.

Document 3

CLASSIFIED ADVERTISING *Double linespacing except where indicated*

If you are looking to advertise yr goods or services then why not try Life Style magazine? Yr (advert) will be seen by over 150,000 readers each month.

Reader Profile

A leading market research group has rated our reader profile very highly. Our regular readers is in the high spending 35 - 65 age bracket and have interests in holidays, travel, home decoration, and gardening. They tend to have at least one child. At least 40% tell us they shop by mail order on a regular basis. *and are interested in educational matters*

Rates

This section only in single linespacing

We offer very competitive rates with discounts for series bookings. A 1 cm x 3 cm column costs from as little as £75 plus VAT. This is printed in one colour and you will be able to fit approx 20 words into this space. If you book three advertisements you are entitled to a 2.5% discount.

If you require a larger advertiseement, or full colour, please ask our advertising sales team for details. *Emphasise this sentence only*

How to Book

Just call our sales team on 01803 2828393. They will be able to give you advice and take your booking over the telephone. If you prefer, you may fax or email your requirements to us. Bookings must be made 4 weeks prior to publication date.

Payment must be made within 10 (days') of receipt of invoice. You may pay by credit card, debit card or cheque. If you book a series of advertisements then it is poss to set up a direct debit. You will be advised of this opp at the time of booking.

Consolidation practice 2 – Document 1

Our ref RL/JK

Mr Richard Laing
62 Morrison Ave
TUNBRIDGE WELLS
BN20 2PY

Dear Mr Laing

Thank you for yr recent order. The miniature bonsai tree kit has been despatched to you by first class parcel post. This means it will be delivered to you within the next 3 to 5 working days.

We hope you will be delighted with yr bonsai tree kit. It should, with a little care and attention, give you many yrs of pleasure. To ensure yr tree grows correctly, please read the enclosed info sheet.

You may be interested to know that we also offer a range of Oriental plant containers and garden ornaments. These can be viewed on our website. Orders of £50 or more are despatched free of packing and postage charges.

If you would like further info on any of our products please do not hesitate to contact us.

Yrs sncly

Joseph Knight
Customer Services Manager

Document 2

From   Joseph Knight

To   Laverne Redburn

Ref   JK/LR

(This is the memorandum)

We have sold a large number of the miniature b_____ tree kits in recent weeks. This may be because of the prominent position it has on the website. ~~It is fast becoming our best selling item~~ [I received a call yesterday from a journalist. She would like to feature some of our ~~goods~~ items ✓ in↓ Life Style Magazine. This is excellent free publicity for our (bussiness.) The bonsai kit is included with these items. Contact details for our co will be given in the article.

(the shopping section of)

It is poss that we will (recieve) a large number of orders for this item. Please ensure we have a (suficient) amount in stock. As you (is) aware, it can take up to eight weeks for the stock to arrive/ from our suppliers. If we have less than 200 kits in the warehouse then I (recomend) you order more.

Thank you for yr help.

Document 3

Double linespacing except where indicated

INFORMATION SHEET

A bonsai is a miniature tree that has all the characteristics of an old tree that has survived many years. For over 2,000 years the Chinese have created these by collecting small trees from the countryside and training them to resemble full sized trees. To recreate the look of an old, full-sized tree, wires, levers and weights are used to give the artistic principles such as proportion, unity, balance and symmetry.

Choosing a Container

This section only in single linespacing

It is essential that you choose the correct container for growing your bonsai. These can be purchased from m8ost garden centres and nurseries. You must ensure the pot has at least one drainage hole in the bottom. The width of the pot should be approximatley two thirds of the height of the tree. The height of the pot should be approximately one and a half times the diameter of the trunk at the soil level.

Growing Essentials

In order to survive bonsai need all the bassic requirements of any tree, that is water, oxygen, sunlight and nutrients. In this respect, cultivating bonsai is no different to growing any other houseplant.

To ensure the bonsai has sufficient sunlight, it is possible to grow it outdoors from mid-spring to mid-autumn. Obviously the tree will require wat;ering on a regular basis. The general rule is to water ~~when ever~~ whenever the soil is dry. For most, this willl probably be every day during the summer months and every day or second day during spring and autumn. If the tree are kept indoors during the winter months, it is recommended that you water it every other day.

Feeding your tree is also very important. During spring and autumn the tree should be fertilised every two weeks. Ordinary houseplant fertiliser can be used, however you should use only half the recomended strength. During winter, if the tree has been brought indoors, fertilise it approximately every month.

If you follow these guidelines you will enjoy your bonsai tree for many years to come.

Consolidation practice 3 – Document 1

Our ref HC/BJ

Miss Belinda Jones
29 Lavender Rd
PAIGNTON
TQ3 8LJ

Dr Miss Jones

Thank you for yr recent letter. We are pleased to be able to offer you a work exp placement with our co.

This will take place from Mon 22 June until ~~Fri~~ 26 June. Thurs ✓ You will be based at our Torquay office. Please report to the main reception at 9.00 am. Ask for Karen Milne who will be yr supervisor for the period of yr placement.

Phoenix Enterprises are (comitted) to assisting young people in their education. We try to give as many students as poss the chance to exp working for our co. ~~We try to employ the students whenever possible.~~ In order for you to gain the most from yr placement we have written an info sheet. This tells you a (little about ourselves) We hope this will be of interest to you. (and gives you some info on what to do on yr first day.) We look forward to meeting you on the 22 June. If you have any queries, please do not hesitate to contact us.

Yrs sncly

Helga Criss
Human Resources Manager

Document 2

From Helga Criss

To   Karen Milne

This is the memorandum

Ref KM/BJ

Thank you for agreeing to have Belinda J—— as a work placement student. It is very much appreciated. Belinda will be with us for one week, commencing 22 June. I *beleeve* she wishes to have a career in *bussiness* administration when she finishes her studies. She is currently studying office technology and *buseness* administration at college.

I would be grateful if you could ensure Belinda *are* instructed in health and safety matters. She will need to know about the *five procedures and general safety regulations.* *during her first morning with us.*

As part of the course, Belinda will need to show evidence of the work she has undertaken with us. I *beleve* she will have a log or diary that she will complete each day. I would be grateful if you could check and sign this at the end of each ~~working~~ day. At the end of the week you will be asked to complete our standard work placement form.

Belindas' lecturer will be visiting her during her time with us. I will let you know the exact date and time once these *has* been confirmed.

Document 3

WORK PLACEMENT

Phoenix Enterprises ~~are~~ committed to ~~our~~ *its* work placement programme. We hope that you will enjoy working with us during ~~your~~ *the* placement and that you will gain some insight into the world of work. These notes will help you prepare for yr first day.

Preparing for your Placement

Obviously one of the most important factors is that your outfit is clean and tidy. Sensible shoes should be worn. ~~Cosmetics and jewellery must be subtle.~~

It is very useful if you preapre for your work placement in advance. We expect students to dress approprately for the workplace. The dress code for our offices is that men should wear a smart jacket and trousers with tie and shirt. Women may wear a skirt or trousers, with blouse and preferably a jacket.

Another way in which you can prepare for your placement is to find out about Phoenix Enterprises. This will give you some background knowledge and will help you when you are at the office. You can find out about us by looking at our website www.phoenix.com.

Making the Most of Your Placement

It is important that you make the most of yr placement ~~with~~ ~~Phoenix Enterprises~~. It is an opp to find out how the world of work operates. Be punctual every day, be courteous to yr coleagues and show a willingness to learn. If you cannot attend for any reason then please call us before 9.30 am.

The type of work you do will depend on the dept in which you are placed. You will be supervised by a member of staff who will check that you understand what to do. // Remember you are learning all the time and no-one will expect you to be perfect straightaway! Ask lots of questions as this will give you a greater insight into yr role at work.

We hope you enjoy your experience with Phoenix Enterprises.

Taking the examination

This section tells you exactly what the examiner will be looking for when marking your work. It does this by showing you the most common errors in documents submitted for the examination, together with hints on how to resolve these errors.

It also includes two examination practice exercises for you to complete to prepare you for the OCR examination.

Document 1

This document requires you to key in a letter. You may need to indicate an enclosure. The current date must be inserted and you should make the various amendments as indicated in the draft. Remember, you must use headed paper or a headed template for the letter.

Exercise 2.33

Look at the two letters shown below (Figures 2.10 and 2.11). The first is correct, the second contains ten errors. Can you spot them?

Our ref   JP/SB

30.05.03

Mr John Pierce
72 Woodland Park
Keynsham
BRISTOL
BS23 5NE

Dear Mr Pierce

Thank you for your recent letter and completed application form. Unfortunately we are unable to process this request as you have not included proof of your current address.

Please send proof of your address. This could take the form of your current driving licence, utility bill, credit card statement, or council tax bill. You must send the original documents as photocopies will not be accepted.

As soon as we receive this information we will process your request. You will be given our decision within three working days.

We look forward to hearing from you. If you require any further information, please do not hesitate to contact us.

Yours sincerely

Sally Billett
Mortgage Manager

Figure 2.10
Correct version

Our ref   JP/SB

05.30.03

Mr John Pierce
72 Woodland Pk
Keynsham
Bristol
BS23 5NE

Dear Mr John Pierce

Thank you for your recent letter and completed application form.
Unfortunately we are unable to process this request as you have not
included proof of your current address.

Please send proof of your address. This could take the form of your
current driving licence, credit card statement , utility bill, or council tax
bill. You must send the original documents as photocopy's will not be
accepted.

As soon as we receive this info we will process your request. You will be
given our decision within three working days. We look forward to
hearing from you. If you require any further info, please do not hesitate
to contact us.

Yours Sincerely
Sally Billett
Mortgage Manager

Figure 2.11 Incorrect version

Error 1

The date has been inserted in American style, ie the month, then the day and then
the year. This is not acceptable in OCR examinations. The date must be presented in
the following order: day, month, year.

Solution

If you have used the **Insert** function, then you will need to change the format of the
date through this menu. Go to **Insert**, choose **Date and Time** and then look at the
available formats. Ensure that the highlight is on the correct format. It should look
like this:

27 June 2003

Note that there is no punctuation included. Once you have selected the correct day
then click **OK** to close the menu box. You may like to make the English format your
default – that means that the date will always be formatted in the chosen style. To
do this, after highlighting the correct date, choose **Default**. A box will appear asking
you to confirm your choice. Click on **Yes**. Then click **OK** to leave the menu.

Error 2

The abbreviation Pk has been left in the address block.

Solution

You must check your work to ensure that all abbreviations have been expanded. Make sure you learn all the abbreviations given on page 35.

Error 3

The postal town (Bristol) has been keyed in with an initial capital. All post towns must be keyed in using blocked capitals as in example 1.

Solution

Ensure you follow draft very carefully. Proofread before you print your work.

Error 4

The salutation contains the name John.

Solution

Key in text exactly as it is shown on the examination paper (apart from abbreviations and spelling errors). Examination papers usually set out the salutation as 'Dear Mrs Huckrak' or 'Dear Mr Cowan' and leave out the first name, although it almost always appears in the address block.

Error 5

The words 'utility bill' and 'credit card statement' appear in the wrong order and there is a space before the comma.

Solution

This was a transposition correction. You must make sure that you make all the amendments shown. Remember to check that the punctuation is still correct after you have moved text. If it helps, use a pen or highlighter to 'tick off' the amendments as you make them. Proofreading your work will also help to solve this problem.

Error 6

The word 'photocopies' has been keyed in as 'photocopy's'.

Solution

Make sure you are completely familiar with the rules on apostrophes. See page 59 if you need further help. Unless a word is circled as incorrect, do not change words given on the examination paper, even if you think they might be wrong.

Error 7

The abbreviation info has been left in the main text.

Solution

Run the spellchecker to ensure that abbreviations are picked up. This should also help find any spelling or typographical errors that may have been made. You should also ensure that you proofread your work very carefully.

Error 8

Two paragraphs have been joined together.

Solution

You must ensure that the paragraphs are exactly the same as the draft. Even if you think the paragraphing of a document is poor or incorrect, at this level you are not expected to insert your own. It may be that this was an amendment that should have been made. You must proofread your work very carefully before printing.

Error 9

There is a capital 'S' in sincerely. This is a very common error.

Solution

Again, follow draft for capitalisation. Unless a deliberate error (which will be circled at Level 1) has been made (for example a lower case letter beginning a sentence) you will not be penalised for following the draft with regard to capital letters.

Error 10

There is no clear space between Yours sincerely and Sally Billet. This will be penalised in the examination.

Solution

You must ensure that you leave at least one clear line space between the complimentary close and the name. If you haven't enough space left to leave the usual five spaces, it is acceptable to leave just one clear line space.

Document 2

This document requires you to key in a memo. A memo template must be used, or you should set out the memo as shown on page 42. You may need to indicate an enclosure. The current date must be inserted and you should make the various amendments as indicated in the draft.

Exercise 2.34

Look at the two memos shown below (Figures 2.12 and 2.13). The first is correct. The second contains six errors. Can you spot them?

To   Petra Dixon

From   Kate Barrington

Ref   PD/KB

Date   24 June 2003

It has come to my notice that there is very little paper left in the stationery store. Maggie, who normally deals with the stationary order is away for three weeks on annual leave. I would be grateful if you could order more paper and any other supplies that are low immediately.

We will be sending out a large number of letters relating to our advertising campaign next week. It is important that we have sufficient supplies of paper, toner and envelopes.

You should find the relevant information to help you place this order in Maggie's filing cabinet. I am enclosing a list of items I would like ordered. If you have any difficulties please let me know.

Enc

Figure 2.12 Correct version

To   Petra Dixon

From   Kate Barrington

Ref   SS/PD/KB

It has come to my notice that there is very little paper left in the stationary store. Maggie, who normally deals with the stationary order is away for three weeks on annual leave. I would be grateful if you could order more paper and any other supplies that are low immediately. We will be sending out a large number of letters relating to our advertising campaign next week. It is important that we have sufficient supplies of paper, toner and envelopes.

You should find the relevant information to help you place this order in Maggie's filing cabinet. I am enclosing a list of items I would like ordered. If you have any difficulties please let me know.

Kate

Figure 2.13 Incorrect version

Error 1

The candidate's initials have been added to the reference. This will incur a penalty in the examination.

Solution

As with all text processing documents, do not add anything to the examination documents, except for the date and an enclosure indicator, if required.

Error 2

The word stationery has been spelt incorrectly.

Solution

This is a more difficult error to correct as the incorrect spelling of stationary is also a correct word and so you cannot rely on the spellchecker to pick it up. The only solution to this problem is to check your work very carefully against the examination paper.

Error 3

Two paragraphs have been merged together.

Solution

Follow draft carefully to ensure that your paragraphs are exactly the same as the draft.

Error 4

The candidate has added a closure to the memo (Kate). This is not necessary and would incur a penalty in the examination.

Solution

Key in only the text required.

Error 6

The enclosure has not been indicated.

Solution

You must ensure that all enclosures are indicated at the bottom of the text. If you read through the text before you start keying it in, then you will spot that an enclosure needs to be indicated. Write this on the examination paper to remind you.

Document 3

This document requires you to key in an article. You will be expected to keep the layout consistent and to amend the text as indicated. Extra paragraphs of text will be handed to you during the course of the examination and these must be inserted where indicated. A continuation sheet will be required and this must be numbered correctly.

Exercise 2.35

Look at the two articles shown below (Figures 2.14 and 2.15). The first is correct, the second has nine errors. Can you spot them?

SPECIAL OFFERS

Phoenix Sounds are giving away the latest CDs and DVDs at the most amazingly low prices. These offers will last until the end of September. **Hurry down to your nearest store and check out the bargains.**

Phoenix Club Members can claim an extra 5% off the price of any CD or DVD. As an introductory

offer, if you join the Club before the end of September you will be able to take £10 off the price of

a CD or DVD.

Club membership costs just £5 and entitles you to a discount on every item you buy, plus extra offers not available to non-members.

CDs

The top 100 CDs have been reduced by £5. We also have 'two for the price of three' on all your favourite sounds.

DVDs

We guarantee that the latest release DVDs will be offered at a lower price than any of our competitors. Our range of DVDs is the largest in the UK. Come and look at our bargain range which starts from just £5.99.

Figure 2.14 Correct version

Special Offers

Phoenix Sounds are giving away the latest CDs and DVDs at the most amazingly low prices. These offers will last until the end of September. **Hurry down to your nearest store and check out the** bargains.

Phoenix Club Members can claim an extra 5% off the price of any CD or DVD. As an introductory offer, if you join the Club before the end of September you will be able to take £10 off the price of a CD or DVD.

Club membership costs just £5 and entitles you to a discount on every item you buy, plus extra offers not available to non-members.

CDs

The top 100 CDs have been reduced by five pounds. We also have 'two for the price of three' on all your favourite sounds.

DVDs

We guarantee that the latest release DVDs will be offered at a lower price than any of our competitors. Our range of DVDs is the largest in the UK. Come and look at our bargain range which starts from just £5.99.

Figure 2.15 Incorrect version

Error 1

The heading has been displayed in initial capitals.

Solution

You must display headings exactly as indicated on the examination paper. It may be that you will just follow the draft or there may be an instruction that tells you how to display the heading.

Error 2

The last word 'bargains' and the full stop have not been emphasised as requested.

Solution

Make sure that the emphasis is exactly as indicated. Be very careful when highlighting text to add the emphasis as it is easy to miss words.

Error 3

The second paragraph is not in double line spacing.

Solution

This is a very common error. It doesn't matter whether you choose to change the line spacing before you start keying in text or once you have finished. Whichever way you choose to work, make sure you treat the change as an amendment and tick it off your list when you have made the change.

Error 4

The sum of money (five pounds) has been written in words in the CD section. This is an inconsistent display compared to all the other sums of money in the exercise.

Solution

Make sure that you make a note of any times or sums of money etc. in a document. Then choose a method of display and keep to it.

Error 5

There is a much bigger space left between the CD and DVD paragraphs than the others.

Solution

Make sure that you check the paragraphing on screen before you print.

Examination practice

To help you prepare for the examination, three full examination papers follow. Try to complete these in exam conditions. That is, finish in the 1 hour and 15 minutes allowed, including printing. Do not ask for help or refer to this book for information on how to do things. Try not to talk to anyone whilst working on these tasks. If you can do all of these then your work will give you a good indication of whether you are ready to sit the real exam. Once you have completed the tasks, you can check your documents with the worked examples on the CD-ROM.

When you are working through these exercises you will need to remember the following:

- Ensure you have corrected any deliberate errors including errors of agreement.
- If you are unsure of a spelling that has been circled as incorrect, use a dictionary as well as the spellchecker.
- Remember to spellcheck your work after you have finished each document.
- Consistency is very important. Make sure that all your work, including spacing between paragraphs, numbers etc. shows a consistent display.
- Enclosures must be indicated and continuation sheets numbered.
- When checking details from one document to another, you must ensure the details you key in are absolutely correct.
- Once you have finished keying in the text for a document, check with the exam paper that you have not keyed in the same word or line twice, or that you have not missed a word or line. These are very common errors and can lose you a large number of marks.

If you can complete all the work within the time and without too many errors then you should now try working on some past examination papers. These will give you a feel for the type of examination paper you are likely to face. You must not become too complacent, even if you are consistently doing well in practice papers, as the examination can make you nervous and this is when it is easy to make mistakes.

The key to success in the examination is proofreading your work carefully, referring back to the examination paper to check that you have keyed in the correct words, not the ones you think are there or should be there!

Examination practice 1 – Document 1

Our ref JM/RH

Mrs Jennie Mitchell
194 Meadow Croft Drive
MANCHESTER
M39 1SP

Dr Mrs Mitchell

Further to our recent telephone conversation, we have now visited Sea View Cottage as requested. We (is) pleased to say that we feel this cottage would make an excellent holiday home.

It (have) lovely sea views and the (acomodasion) is beautifully decorated and presented. (in the high season) We (beleve) the rental for this cottage should be in the region of £480 per week. A cottage of this type will let for approx 24 (week's) of the yr. If you are prepared to allow guests to bring their dog then this will help to fill the property outside of the high season. An info sheet giving details of our services is enclosed. Please read this carefully and then contact us if you have any further questions.

We look forward to letting Sea View Cottage on yr behalf.

Yrs sncly

Robert Haynes
Manager

Document 2

From   Robot Haynes

To   Laura Nugent

This is the memorandum

Ref   RH/LN/JM

I have written to Mrs Mitchell regarding Sea View Cottage. I suggested a rental of £___ per week during the high season. This compares well with West Quay Cottage and Cutlass Cottage, both of which can sleep four people. // I am sure this will prove to be a very popular cottage with our guests. It has recently been redecorated and has a have two bedrooms and garage. The sea views are outstanding.

The owner will ~~provide~~ give us with some photographs for the ✓ website. As soon as these have been received I would like you to draft ~~prepare~~ a new page for this property. I will prepare some details for you to use within the next few days.

Unfortunately, I have received a letter from Mr Green, the owner of Mermaid Cottage. He is planning to sell the property in the autumn. This means we cannot take any bookings after the end of September. I have looked at the forward bookings and this should not cause us any problems.

Please ensure that all call centre staff are aware of the situation. I would also like you to remove this propertys details from the website.

Document 3

Use double linespacing

LETTING YOUR PROPERTY

Thank you for choosing Phoenix Holidays to let yr holiday home. Given below is some info which we hope you will find useful.

Property Standards

an excellent

The property must be of a good standard for our guests and this includes furnishings, bedding, and electrical appliances. Our property standard booklet will be sent to you upon receipt of your signed agreeement.

soft

However, you should bear in mind that all furnishings must comply with current fire safety regulations. A gas safety certificate must be issued yearly if appropriate.

Emphasise this word

Cleaning

It is essential that each property is thoroughly cleaned between lets. If you are unable to find a housekeeper then we can organise the cleaning for you. This incurs a seperete charge of approx £25 per week. This charge includes cleaning materials.

This paragraph in single linespacing

Payment

in arrears

Rental income due to you will be paid directly into your bank account one month after the booking has taken place. Payment is made on the 28 of each month. Deductions for cleaning, approved repairs and maintenance will be made from the gross income. A statement will be sent to you on a monthly basis. This will itemize all payments made and receeved.

Cancelling yr Contract

Once you have signed an agreement, you are bound to let yr property for a period of 12 months. Unfortunately, because we cannot cancel holidays, you will be unable to take possession of yr property until the agreement has expired. Please bear this in mind when considering a holiday let.

Examination practice 2 – Document 1

Our ref NE/CH

Mrs Natalie Elliott
145 Beauchamp Ave
CHELTENHAM
Glos
GL3 8NQ

Dr Mrs Elliott

Thank you for bringing in yr dresses for us to sell at the Dress Exchange. I would like to confirm that all items have now been sold. // A cheque for £322 is enclosed with this letter. This is the payment due to you after our commission of 25% has been deducted.

We (was) able to sell all the garments at the agreed price and no reductions were necy.

At our last meeting you said that you would ~~probably~~ definitely ✓ be sending more items for us to sell. We would be very pleased to accept these. Unfortunately, however, we will not be able to take any more stock for the next four week's. This is because we will be closing temp in order for the shop to be refurbished. [We will write to you again when we are re-open for busness. ⌐Subject to the usual terms and conditions

Yrs sncly

Charmaine Hamilton
Manager

Document 2

From   Charmaine Hamilton   This is the
To   Polly Folkes   memorandum

Ref   PF/CH

I have just received a telephone call from Harold Amers. He is the manager of the co that will be refurbishing the shop next month. He told me that planning permission has now been granted. This means we can extend the size of the ~~shop~~ window as planned. This is ~~very~~ ① good news.

In light of this, the refurbishment will take a full three weeks. This means the shop will be closed for a total of four weeks. This depends of course on the building works finishing on schedule. ~~Most building works over-run in my experience.~~ [I was wondering whether it might be a good idea to rent the empty shop further down the High Street for this period. This would be a great help. It would give us somewhere to store our stock and we could also open for business. Please let me have ~~know~~ yr thoughts as soon as possible.

I will speak to the commercial agent and see if it would be possable to rent the shop for such a short period. in the meantime

Document 3

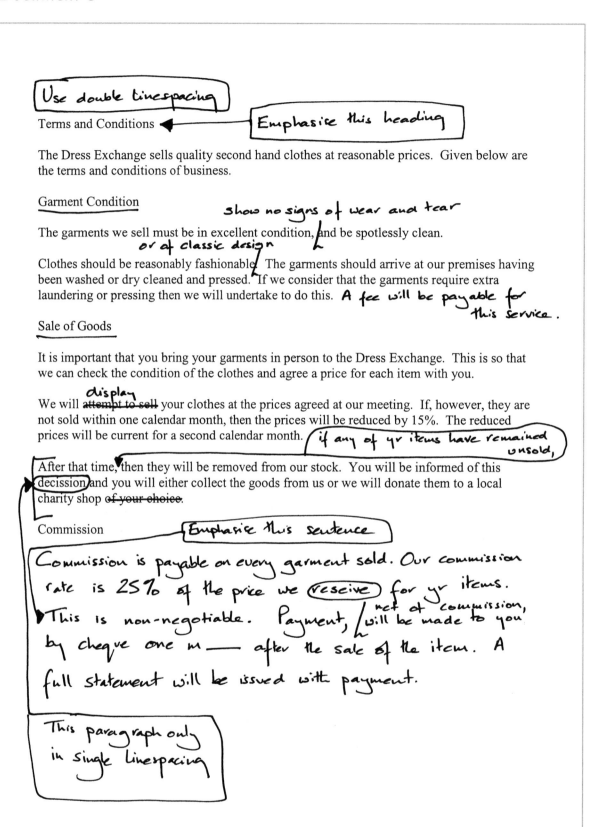

Use double linespacing

Terms and Conditions ← *Emphasise this heading*

The Dress Exchange sells quality second hand clothes at reasonable prices. Given below are the terms and conditions of business.

Garment Condition

show no signs of wear and tear

The garments we sell must be in excellent condition, and be spotlessly clean.

or of classic design

Clothes should be reasonably fashionable. The garments should arrive at our premises having been washed or dry cleaned and pressed. If we consider that the garments require extra laundering or pressing then we will undertake to do this. *A fee will be payable for this service.*

Sale of Goods

It is important that you bring your garments in person to the Dress Exchange. This is so that we can check the condition of the clothes and agree a price for each item with you.

display

We will ~~attempt to sell~~ your clothes at the prices agreed at our meeting. If, however, they are not sold within one calendar month, then the prices will be reduced by 15%. The reduced prices will be current for a second calendar month. *if any of yr items have remained unsold,*

After that time, then they will be removed from our stock. You will be informed of this *decission* and you will either collect the goods from us or we will donate them to a local charity shop ~~of your choice~~.

Commission *Emphasise this sentence*

Commission is payable on every garment sold. Our commission rate is 25% of the price we receive for yr items. This is non-negotiable. Payment, net of commission, will be made to you by cheque one m___ after the sale of the item. A full statement will be issued with payment.

This paragraph only in single linespacing

Examination practice 3 – Document 1

Our ref KV/SG

Ms Kathy Vesey
Flat 8B
Park Cres
SWINDON
SN12 6DJ

Dr Ms Vesey

Thank you for yr article, submitted last week. We found it very interesting and feel it is suitable for publication. It will be published in our special Valentine's issue. This goes on sale on the 2 Feb.

The usual short article fee are payable and you should receive this within 14 days of the date of this letter.

We would like to commission you to write a series of articles for LifeStyle Magazine. The articles should be on the subject of high flying busines women. It would be particularly interesting if you could find women who have worked their way up the career ladder. Another idea is that the women may have drastically changed their career path before becoming very successful.

If you would like to write this series then please call me as soon as poss. We can then arrange to meet and discuss the matter further. Payment can also be discussed at the meeting.

Yrs sncly

Simone Greene
Features Editor

Document 2

This is the memorandum

From Simone Greene

To Anu Sharma

Ref SG/AS

Please find attached the article for the Valentines' issue written by Kathy V____ . The magazine will go on sale on 2 Feb. I would be grateful if you could arrange payment for Kathy. The usual short article fee applies.

I think Kathy is a very talented ~~writer~~ author and ✓ would like to commission her more often. I have asked her if she would like to write a series of article's for us in the near future.

If Kathy is interested in writing these articles she will contact me to arrange a meeting. if at all poss I would like you to be present at this meeting. ~~Let me know the dates you are available~~

The subject matter is successful busness women who have worked their way to the top of their profession. I think this will make interesting and ~~hopefully~~ inspiring reading.

Document 3

VALENTINE'S DAY [①] Double linespacing except where indicated.

The tradition of sending tokens of affection and love on St Valentine's Day is a very ~~ancient~~ *old* one. Pope Gelasius set aside 14 February as the day to honour St Valentine as long ago as 496 AD.

Interesting Facts

the oldest known Valentine

A poem sent by Charles, Duke of Orleans to his wife in 1415 is / still in existence. The poem is part of the manuscript (colllection) at the British Library.

By the middle of the eighteenth century it was common for friends and lovers to exchange small tokens of affection or handwritten notes. By the end of the century printed cards could be purchased and these began to replace handwritten letters.

→ It is (estim6ated) that one billion Valentine cards (is) sent each year, eighty five per cent of which are purchased by women.

Emphasise this sentence only

Strange Traditions

In the middle ages, young men and women would draw a name from bowl to see who their Valentine would be. The piece (fo) paper would be pinned to their sleeve.

This practice coined the phrase 'to wear your heart on your sleeve'.

It used to be (beleived) that if a woman saw a robin flying overhead on Valentine's Day it would mean she would marry a sailor. If she saw a goldfinch she would marry a wealthy man, however if she saw a sparrow she would marry a poor man - but be very happy.

eating

An old tradition for Valentine's Day was to cut an / apple in half and count the number of seeds. This would tell you how many children you were likely to have.

This section only in single linespacing

Part 3

Word processing

The Level 1 Word Processing examination consists of three documents, three of which you recall from the computer or disk. The three documents are:

1 An article or report
2 A notice for display
3 A three column table with headings

You are allowed 1 hour and 30 minutes in which to complete the examination.

You will be asked to demonstrate a number of skills, by using the keyboard and your knowledge and application of English. Each of the three tasks will contain one or more of the following:

- Emphasis of text
- Amendments using correction signs
- Information which must be keyed in using a consistent format
- A continuation sheet
- Changing the alignment of the text, the line spacing and the line length
- Displaying information in tabular format
- Insetting text from the margin(s)

In this section you will learn about the following:

- Multi-page articles or reports
- Notice for display
- Three column table
- Consolidation practice
- Taking the examination

Multi-page articles or reports

This is slightly different to the article contained in the Text Processing examination as the majority of the text is already keyed in and saved to disk. Your task is to amend the text as indicated on the examination paper, including keying in more text. The type of amendments you will be expected to make are as follows:

- Adjust the line length of the document.
- Change the text alignment. Information on text alignment can be found on page 21.

- Change the line spacing from single to double or vice versa. Instructions for this can be found on page 9.
- Emphasise text. Information regarding emphasis can be found on page 55.
- Move text from where it is shown on the examination paper to a new location. Information is given below on how to move text.
- Number a continuation sheet.
- Inset text from margins.

Correcting recalled text

Making corrections to recalled text is different to correcting text as you key it in. You must ensure that you place the cursor exactly where you want to make the correction. Be careful that you do not delete text around the area where you are going to make an amendment.

One way you can ensure that you do not delete or over-write existing text is to check that the over-write facility is switched off. This facility is shown at the bottom of the toolbar by the initials **OVR**. This should be 'ghosted', that is it should be in grey writing. If it is in bold then double click on it to switch it off.

When you make a correction, you must ensure that you do not add or delete spaces between characters, words or punctuation. If at all possible, print out a copy of your work and check it before the examination finishes. If you have made any mistakes you will be able to spot them easily and will be able to correct them before the final printing.

The information given below will help you when making corrections to existing text.

Inserting and deleting page breaks

The easiest and safest way of inserting and deleting page breaks is as follows:

Method

1 Bring up the 'hidden' codes by pressing the **Show/Hide** icon which should be on your toolbar. ¶
2 Depending on how the file has been constructed you will either see a line space mark ¶ or the words 'page break'. To **Delete**, highlight the mark or words and press **Delete**.
3 To insert a page break, hold down **Ctrl** and press **return**. A new page break will be inserted.

Run on

The correction sign for running on text is:

If you are asked to run two paragraphs together you will need to place your cursor immediately before the first word of the second paragraph. Use the **backspace** key to delete the line space and to move the second paragraph to the end of the first paragraph. Remember that you must leave the same number of spaces after the full stop as you usually do when keying in text.

Deleting and inserting hard returns

You may find that you need to delete or insert a hard return especially where you have moved text or run on two paragraphs. You can do this by placing the cursor at the end of the extra line space that you wish to delete, or at the beginning of the line of text you wish to move down, and using the **backspace** key to move the text accordingly.

Creating a new paragraph

The correction sign for creating a new paragraph is:

If you need to create a new paragraph, you will need to place the cursor immediately before the first word of the paragraph to be created. Press the **return** key to make the required number of clear line spaces. If you do not do this accurately and create an extra space at the beginning of the new paragraph, use the **backspace** key to delete it.

Deleting words or sentences

If you have to delete a word or sentence, then you will need to highlight the existing text. You can do this by placing the cursor inside the word and double clicking it. The entire word will be highlighted and you can then press **Delete** to remove the word.

To delete a sentence you will also need to highlight the words, but do ensure that you only highlight exactly what you need. This is slightly more difficult than deleting a word as you must make sure you do not delete too many or too few spaces on either side. If you are not sure then use the Show/Hide icon on the toolbar.

Deleting and replacing words or sentences

When replacing words or sentences with new text, the easiest way to do this is to highlight the text that you wish to delete and then type in the new words. You will then automatically delete the text you do not want.

Adjusting the line length

You will be required to recall a document from a disk, file or CD and change the margins to a specified line length. It is very important that you remember to change all the text contained within the document and that text you add to the document is also at the new line length.

Recall the document called Cosmetics from the CD-ROM and change the line length to 12 cm.

Method

1   Check that the measurements for your document are in cm. To do this go to **Tools** and choose **Options**. Click on the **General** tab and the following menu will appear (Figure 3.1).

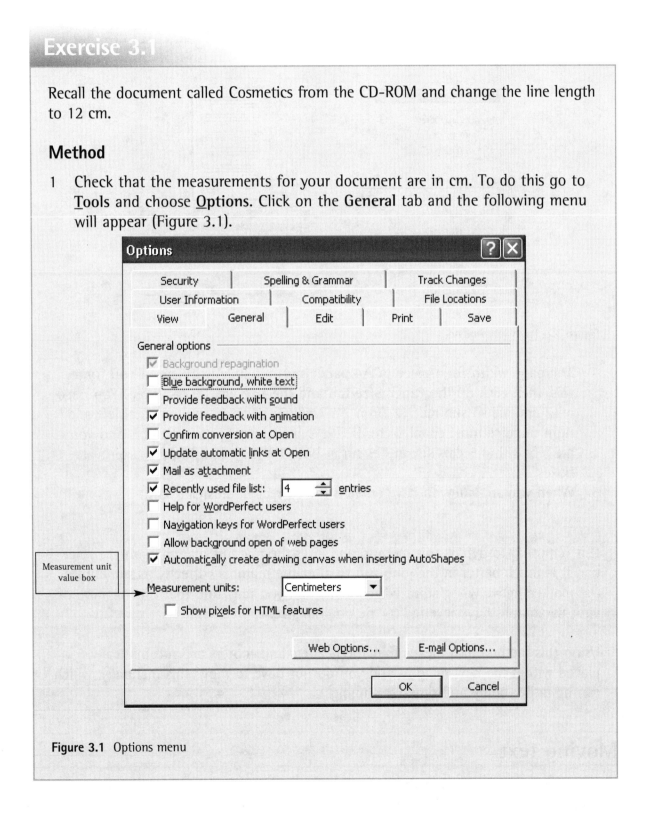

Measurement unit value box

Figure 3.1 Options menu

2   Check that the value in the <u>M</u>easurement units box is set to centimetres. If it is not, then using the drop down to the right-hand side, change the value. Click **OK**.

3   Now go to <u>F</u>ile and choose Page Set<u>u</u>p. The following menu will appear (Figure 3.2):

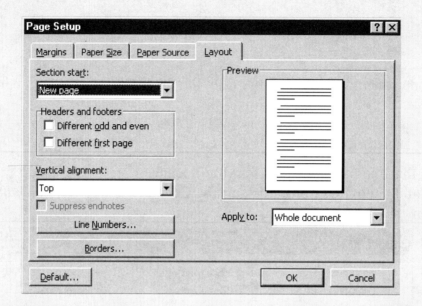

Figure 3.2 Page Setup menu

4   The page width for a piece of A4 paper, portrait style is 21 cm. If you forget this, then click on the **Paper <u>S</u>ize** tab and the size will be displayed. You need a 12 cm line so subtract 12 from 21. This gives you 9, so your total left and right margins must equal 9 cm. Divide 9 by 2 to get equal margins and you are left with 4.5 cm. Key in 4.5 cm in both the **Le<u>f</u>t** and **Rig<u>h</u>t** margin value boxes.

5   When you are sure you have entered the correct figures click **OK**.

NOTE

It is tempting to bypass this method and alter the margins manually on the ruler bar. It is much better in the long run to alter the margins correctly as sometimes the markers move when adjusted manually and you may find that one or more of your paragraphs have reverted to the original size.

Using this method also means that the headers and footers are automatically placed within the new margins and you do not have to move this manually, which can be rather fiddly and time-consuming.

Moving text

The important thing to remember when you are moving text is that the block of text should only appear *once* in the document. This means that the text should be taken from one location and placed in a different location.

Exercise 3.2

Recall the document Cosmetics from the CD-ROM. Move the paragraph that begins 'Women felt confident ...' so that it becomes the fourth paragraph of the document.

Method 1

1 Highlight the entire paragraph by treble clicking on the text.
2 Hold down the **Ctrl** key and press X. The text should disappear.
3 Move to the correct new location and click so that the cursor is flashing.
4 Hold down the **Ctrl** key and press V. The text should now appear.
5 Ensure that there is a clear line space above and below the moved paragraph.

Method 2

1 Highlight the entire paragraph by treble clicking on the text.
2 Go to **E**dit and choose **Cut**. The text should disappear.
3 Move to the correct new location and click so that the cursor is flashing.
4 Go to **E**dit and choose **P**aste. The text should now appear.
5 Ensure that there is a clear line space above and below the moved paragraph.

Inset text from margins

Insetting text from margins means that the text is indented either from the left or both margins. This is often used to make a display feature. Look at the example below.

> This text has been inset 2 cm from both margins and makes a display feature. By insetting the margins correctly the text will remain in neat lines. If you do not use the given method but use the tab key, you may find there are problems if you have to amend the text at a later stage.

Recall the document called Cosmetics from the CD rom. Inset the paragraph beginning 'Women have worn cosmetics...' 2 cm from the left margin.

Method

1 Highlight the text you wish to indent.
2 Go to **F<u>o</u>rmat** and choose **<u>P</u>aragraph**. The following menu will appear (Figure 3.3).

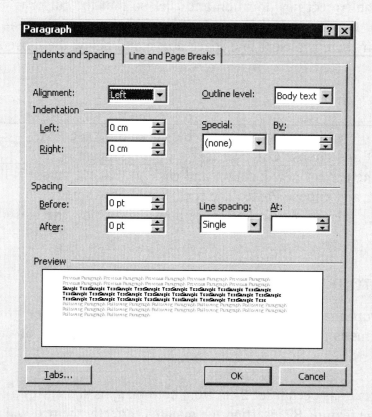

Figure 3.3 Paragraph menu

3 Make sure the **<u>I</u>ndents and Spacing** tab is uppermost.
4 In the **<u>L</u>eft** value box, key in the amount of cm you wish to indent. In this instance it will be 2 cm.
5 When you are sure you have completed the boxes correctly, click **OK**.

Note: This is the best way of indenting text, as if you make any changes or move paragraphs of text then the indent will remain in place.

Numbering continuation sheets

Whenever you use a second page either in a letter, memo or article, the second and subsequent pages should always be numbered. Word has an automatic page numbering facility that you can use.

Exercise 3.4

Using the recalled document Cosmetics, make the following amendments. Insert a page number on the second and any subsequent pages. Please use double line spacing, except where indicated, and a justified right-hand margin. A correct version appears in the worked examples on the CD-ROM.

> Recall this document stored under Exercise 3.4. Amend as shown. Change to double linespacing (except where indicated). Adjust the line length to 12 cm. Use a justified right margin. Save as COSMETICS and print one copy.

COSMETICS

Inset this paragraph 20 mm from left margin

Women have worn cosmetics to improve their appearance for many years. It is well documented that in Elizabethan times women, and men, used a mixture of lead, flour and water to give themselves a deathly white appearance. This sometimes resulted in death to the user, as lead is highly toxic.

Since the 1900s, cosmetics have changed dramatically both in ~~the attitudes of society and in~~ the physical product. In 1900 cosmetics were viewed as worn only by music hall performers and prostitutes. *and the attitude of society toward them*

In fact they were so frowned upon that a gentleman could divorce his wife if she persisted in using cosmetics. To make up for this lack of beauty enhancement, women had very elaborate hairstyles. The Marcel wave, a method of making hair look like a rippling sheet of silk was introduced in this decade.

This paragraph in single linespacing

During 1910 - 1920 Selfridges decided to sell cosmetics (openly) to women. This proved to be very popular ~~with women~~ although it was still frowned upon by many/men. However, after the First World War, when women over 30 were finally given the right to vote, the wearing of cosmetics became widespread.

(*)

During the 1930s and 40s there were two major influences on cosmetics. The first was the increasing world of cinema and celebrities. Hollywood stars influenced the way women wanted to look, rather like the stars of today.

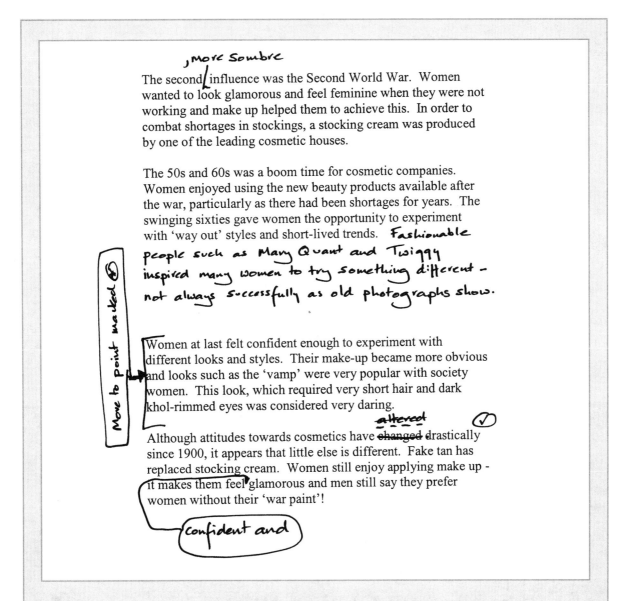

The second, ⟨more sombre⟩ influence was the Second World War. Women wanted to look glamorous and feel feminine when they were not working and make up helped them to achieve this. In order to combat shortages in stockings, a stocking cream was produced by one of the leading cosmetic houses.

The 50s and 60s was a boom time for cosmetic companies. Women enjoyed using the new beauty products available after the war, particularly as there had been shortages for years. The swinging sixties gave women the opportunity to experiment with 'way out' styles and short-lived trends. ⟨Fashionable people such as Mary Quant and Twiggy inspired many women to try something different – not always successfully as old photographs show.⟩

⟨Move to point marked ✐⟩

Women at last felt confident enough to experiment with different looks and styles. Their make-up became more obvious and looks such as the 'vamp' were very popular with society women. This look, which required very short hair and dark khol-rimmed eyes was considered very daring.

Although attitudes towards cosmetics have ~~changed~~ ⟨altered⟩ drastically since 1900, it appears that little else is different. Fake tan has replaced stocking cream. Women still enjoy applying make up – it makes them feel glamorous and men still say they prefer women without their 'war paint'!

⟨confident and⟩

Method

1 Go to **Insert** and choose **Page Numbers**. The following dialogue box will appear on screen.

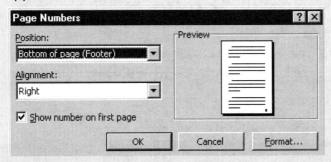

Figure 3.4 Page numbers menu

2 Ensure that the **Show number on first page** box is clear (no tick appears).
3 Check that the page number is set to start at the **Bottom of page (Footer)**. If it is not then click on the arrow to see the various options.
4 Click **OK**.

Exercise 3.5

Using the recalled document Exercise 3.5, make the following amendments. A correct version appears in the worked examples on the CD-ROM.

Recall this document stored under Exercise 3.5. Amend as shown. Use double linespacing (except where indicated). Adjust the line length to 11 cm. Use a justified right margin. Save as MENU and print one copy.

A La Carte ← Emphasise this heading

excavating

Sir William Cristal, when ~~discovering~~ the pyramid containing the tomb of ✓ an Egyptian prince in 1922, found the earliest known menu. This menu, written in hieroglyphics on stone tablets *listed* ~~gave~~ the ~~menu~~ *dishes* for a meal celebrating the birth of *his* twin sons. The dishes comprised of two starters: garlic in sour cream and barley soup; one fish course of salmon and a main course of roast pig and goats cheese. To follow this meal, honey, dates and pomegranates were served.

Move to point marked

Today's menus are often works of art in themselves. Each ingredient is faithfully listed as an essential part of the dish. The descriptions are contrived to make your mouth water. Unfortunately, the meals do not always live up to their publicity.

The menu was in fact a list of instructions for the chef. The order of the dishes was written down for the staff to follow. This was in fact the case with menus until the end of the 18 century. It was important for staff to know what and when to cook as meals were very elaborate and often consisted of many courses.

large

Each course could also consist of a number of different dishes. One 18 century menu listed eight courses, each of which consisted of at least six different dishes. There were eight soups, fourteen roasts and twelve salads.

After consuming these delights, a guest at this dinner party was then expected to work their way through sixteen desserts. Accepting dinner party invitations was obviously not for the faint hearted!

Guests were not expected to choose their meal, but to sample a little of every single dish.

At the time, public eating places ~~such as hotels and inns~~ did not give customers a choice of meals. The owner or chef would devise a menu and that is what was served. Waiters would not necessarily know what was on the menu until the dishes were taken to the guests. Towards the end of the century however, chefs decided that they would give their customers a choice and the practice of writing the daily menu on a chalkboard began.

Famous artists often illustrated menus for their favourite restaurants. Toulouse Lautrec, Renoir and Matisse are amongst those who used their skills in this way. No doubt they received a free meal for their efforts - often welcome to struggling artists. Today these menus are highly sought after, valuable works of art.

Once individual menus became fashionable, eating houses tried different methods to ensure that their menu was artistic and interesting. One restaurant designed a menu that was twenty two pages long. Another designed a menu only six pages long but it was embossed in gold and bound in silver.

drawn up
The longest menu was probably ~~drafted~~ in New Jersey. Over fify starters, forty soups, two hundred salads and four hundred main courses were included. The shortest known menu was a blank sheet of paper handed to Lord and Lady Halifax on the day the chef resigned.

Exercise 3.6

Using the recalled document Exercise 3.6, make the following amendments. A correct version appears in the worked examples on the CD-ROM.

> Recall this document stored under Exercise 3.6. Amend as shown. Change to double linespacing (except where indicated). Adjust the line length to 12 cm. Use a justified right margin. Save as Website and print one copy.

WEBSITE DESIGN ◄——— Centre this heading

With the increasing access and popularity of the Internet, many people have enjoyed building their own website, whether for business purposes or just for pleasure. ~~Some provide step-by-step guides to the design process.~~ There are many different software packages available that are specifically designed for building websites. Once you have finished the design, the software package will help you publish it on the web. ~~Then thousands of people will have the chance to view your site.~~

If you are building a website for a business you will want to ensure that you attract as many people as possible to your site. Once on the site, it must be interesting and attractive *to viewers*. The tips given below should help you ensure that your site is functional, attractive and interesting.

When designing your site you must think about your target audience. Remember that many people do not have fast modems or Broadband connections. *Your site should be configured so that the download time is as fast as possible, taking into account the range of modems that will be used. If your site takes too long to download the viewer may become bored and move onto a different site. Your aim should be to ensure that everything on the page downloads in less than one minute.*

Moving about the site should be easy and efficient. Make sure you have links on every single page so that visitors can navigate the site efficiently. The names of your pages should closely relate to the contents. There is nothing worse than clicking on a link and then finding you cannot get back to the home page or index.

> Move to point marked ◉

This paragraph only in single linespacing

The most time consuming items to download are graphic images and photographs. In order to ensure that these take as little time as possible you will need a good photo editing software package.

These will provide a condensing facility which will enable you to save your images and photographs into the smallest possible format. This can save literally minutes in download time.

fun

Although music and animation may seem ~~interesting~~, if you are looking at a site for business purposes, these will be distracting and irritating. Keep Flash elements and music to an absolute minimum. Many people view sites purely to find out information quickly. They will not want to waste time waiting for the animation to appear.

In order to ensure your visitors come back to your site again and again, make sure you include full information on how to contact you, what you offer and most importantly, where you offer it. It is very annoying to find exactly what you want on a website only to discover it is not possible to obtain the goods or service in your area.

There are a number of specialist courses being held at local colleges and training attending providers. If you are serious about building an efficient, well presented website, ~~this~~ one may be a very good investment of your time and money.

Exercise 3.7

Using the recalled document Exercise 3.7, make the following amendments. A correct version appears in the worked examples on the CD-ROM.

Recall this document stored under Exercise 3.7. Amend as shown. Change to double linespacing (except where indicated). Use a justified right margin. Save as Enterprise and print one copy.

Young Enterprise ← *Emphasise this heading*

The Young Enterprise Programme is an educational charity founded *a few years ago* to form links between schools and industry.

The programme aims to help young people learn about the world of work, *They will* and to also develop attitudes and skills for personal success, lifelong learning and employability through the real experience of running their own business over one academic year.

Move to point marked ⊗

If required, a short examination can be taken which formalises the effort and dedication shown by the students. A worthwhile qualification can be obtained at the same time as the students enjoy themselves, learn new skills and hopefully make some money. A brilliant idea. ✓

businesses
Students form small companies and elect their own board of directors. They then have to raise their own share capital in order to start the company. Just as with a real company, the students have to research their markets, decide on how to operate the business, and finally sell the goods or services they have decided to offer. *Organise production if necessary*

This paragraph in single linespacing

Once money has been made, then students must keep records of income and expenditure, and prepare an annual report. After the year has been completed then the company is wound up and, if the company has been successful, dividends paid to shareholders. *produce profit and loss accounts*
The amount of the dividend depends on the amount of money made.

Students will learn many skills through the Young Enterprise Programme. They will find out how to make and carry through decisions, have develop the ability to be flexible when dealing with others, interpersonal skills, communication skills, creativity, planning, self-discipline and confidence to name a few.

Some students run very successful companies which continue after their one year Young Enterprise programme. A few entrepreneurs have come up with some good ideas that have been well received. by businesses and customers alike.

As well as the enjoyment of running a business, students also get the chance to compete in regional competitions. At these the companies are expected to give a presentation explaining why their business should be considered the best. If successful at the regional level, then a company can go on to compete in national and even international competitions.

Exercise 3.8

Using the recalled document Exercise 3.8, make the following amendments. A correct version appears in the worked examples on the CD-ROM.

Recall this exercise stored under Exercise 3.8. Amend as shown. Change to double linespacing (except where indicated). Amend the line length to 10 cm. Use a justified right margin. Save as BATH and print one copy.

ROMAN BATH ← Centre this heading

The Roman ruins *Remains* found in Bath are probably the most important in Great *Britain* Brittan. The remains are extensive and although much is still buried under the Georgian streets of Bath, there is a great deal that has been excavated, and is now on display to the general public.

It was first discovered by Bladud, the eldest son of a renowned Celtic king. Bladud had suffered from leprosy and was exiled from his home.

Whilst living as a swineherd he noticed that his pigs enjoyed wallowing in hot black mud. When they emerged from the mud their scurvy had been cured.

Legend has it that Bladud *then* also tried bathing in the mud and that his leprosy was *also* cured. He returned to his father's kingdom and later became himself king. In gratitude he built a temple by the hot spring and founded the City of Bath. It was not long Before long the healing powers of the water *became* was known far and wide. Many pilgrims made the *long and arduous* journey to Bath to cure themselves of various ailments. These included leprosy, skin diseases and stomach complaints.

move to point marked (A).

Bath or Aquae Sulis as it was known, was the obvious place to build a large bathing and entertainment complex as it had a natural spring providing hot water.

When the Romans arrived they built their own temple on the same site and blended the goddess Sul with one of their own goddesses Minerva to become Sulis Minerva. The Romans also believed that the goddess guarded the entrance to the underworld.

The Celts believed that the underworld could be reached through gateways such as the hot spring. They worshipped the goddess Sul as the guardian of this underworld.

It was also widely believed that you could communicate directly with the underworld by ~~giving~~ *making an offering to the spring. Almost 20,000 coins together with gold and silver artefacts have been recovered in the area.*

and was contained in its own hall

As well as a temple, the Romans built a bathing complex. This consisted of five hot baths, sweat rooms and cold rooms. The Great Bath was placed at the centre of the complex. The sweat rooms were heated by a hypocaust heating system - a very elaborate feat of engineering. *The remains of these can still be seen today.*

This paragraph only in single linespacing

The Roman Bath's have survived remarkably well. The Great Bath can still be visited and until the 1970s members of the public were able to take a dip and enjoy the healing powers of the hot spring as many thousands of people had before them.

Although it is not possible to swim in the Great Bath these days, a new spa complex has been opened in Bath so that people of today can enjoy the restoring powers of the hot spring.

Emphasise these words

Exercise 3.9

Using the recalled document Exercise 3.9, make the following amendments. A correct version appears in the worked examples on the CD-ROM.

Recall this document stored under Exercise 3.9.
Amend as shown. Change to double linespacing
(except where indicated). Adjust the line length
to 11 cm. Use a justified right margin.
Save as HOME and print one copy.

SELLING YOUR HOME ◄——— Centre this heading

There are a large number of 'home interest' programmes
on the television that show you how to present your home
~~for selling.~~ to potential buyers Although these programmes sometimes
take the idea to the extreme, there are a few
points worth considering when selling your
property.

Move to point marked →

Although it may seem strange to redecorate your property
before you sell it, you can be assured that by spending
money on your home and presenting it well you will
achieve the sale. This means you will be able to move to
your next property in the shortest possible time.

First impressions mean a great deal to a buyer. The
exterior of your property must be clean and tidy. If you
have a front garden make sure that it is free of weeds and
litter.

Plants should be attractive and healthy looking. The front
door should look pristine - polish the letterbox, make sure
the bell is working and if necessary give the front door a
fresh lick of paint. Your windows should ~~shine~~ sparkle and
curtains should be kept open during daylight hours.

The entrance hall is also very important and often overlooked. Do not allow coats, shoes and bags to be cluttering up the entrance hall. As viewers walk into your property they should immediately be impressed. If you cannot afford to redecorate the rooms and replace the carpets then make sure the house is very clean + tidy.

own a

Nowadays many people have computers and use one of the living rooms as a home office. This can be very off-putting for potential buyers. You must ensure that each room has a purpose in the house and furnish it accordingly. The living room must be just that, no clutter, clean and tidy, it should be a room in which the whole family can relax.

The secret of successful selling is to make sure that the viewer can picture themselves living in your home. The house should be rather impersonal so that people can image their own belongings in the room.

When selling your home, keep to the idea that 'less is more'. If you have a collection of soft toys or fancy china plates, this may be very off-putting to potential buyers. The fewer personal items you have lying around the more attractive your home will seem. Clear away your collections of things and any excess equipment, books, cds etc. Keep just one or two carefully selected ornaments and pictures in each room. If possible, co-ordinate the colours of your bedlinen and curtains etc. If at all possible, keep carpets a neutral shade.

You can employ the services of a stylist who will visit your property and make suggestions as to how to present it to its best advantage. It is likely that the stylist will suggest you redecorate some of the rooms, repair or replace broken items + have new carpet fitted. They will also show you how to arrange the furniture and ornaments to make your home as stylish and inviting as possible.

Exercise 3.10

Using the recalled document Exercise 3.10, make the following amendments. A correct version appears in the worked examples on the CD-ROM.

Recall this document stored under Exercise 3.10. Amend as shown. Change to double linespacing (except where indicated). Adjust the line length to 10 cm. Use a justified right margin. Save as GARDEN and print one copy.

GARDEN DESIGN

Garden design has become very popular in recent years and many people have found they enjoy pottering around in their gardens. The benefits to this interesting hobby are many. *You will become fitter, spend more time outdoors and learn new skills. You will also be able to enjoy the fruits of your labour, either by eating the produce you have grown or by just sitting and relaxing in beautiful surroundings.* (*Emphasise these words*)

Inset this paragraph 20 mm from left margin

It doesn't matter whether you have a large ~~half-acre~~ plot or just a small patio or window box. You can still enjoy your garden and spend time planning its design for each season's display. However, before you start gardening there are one or two points you must take into consideration.

You will need to determine

Soil. ~~First of all you should~~ ~~find out~~ the type of soil you have in your garden. The amount of lime contained in the soil will ~~determine~~ *is important as it* whether it is acid or alkaline. This has an effect on the type of plants you will be able to grow successfully.

North

Climate. If you live in the ~~south~~ of Scotland, the type of plants you will be able to grow will differ from those reared in the south west of England. When choosing plants for your garden you must ensure that they are suitable for your climate. If you are planning on keeping a plant over winter then you must ensure that the care label states it is a 'hardy' plant.

Soil testing kits are available from garden centres and nurseries and are easy to use.

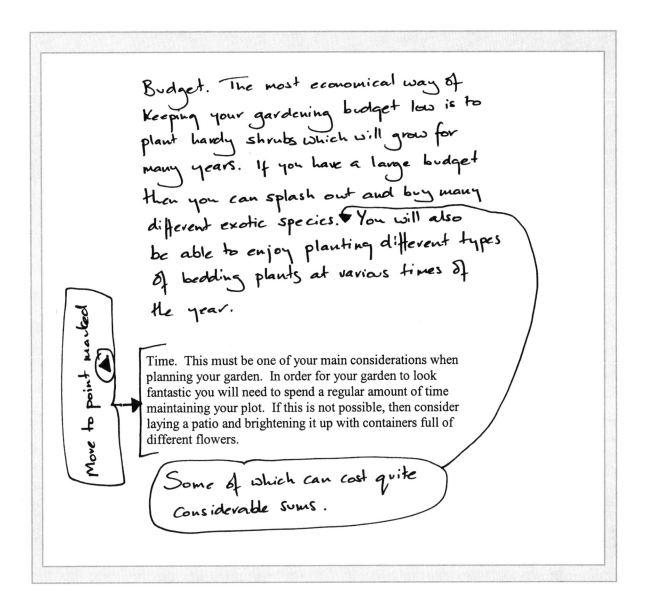

Notice for display

The second task of the word processing examination is a notice for display. This is a recalled document from disk and you will be expected to do the following:

- add text to the document
- inset a section of text.

This is a straightforward task with little new theory. You must however take great care with the following:

- Inserting text within the recalled text – make sure you enter new text correctly.
- Insetting paragraphs – make sure you inset the text by exactly the correct amount.
- Making any necessary corrections – for example transposing paragraphs of text.
- Centring and/or emphasising text.

Exercise 3.11

Recall the document called Exercise 3.11 from the CD-ROM. Make the amendments as shown. Save the document as Waiting and print one copy. A correct version appears in the worked examples on the CD-ROM.

Recall this document stored under Exercise 3.11. Amend as shown. Use a ragged or justified right margin. Save as WAITING and print one copy.

WAITING STAFF REQUIRED ← Centre this heading

Would you like to become part of a team? Are you good with people? Do you possess a good sense of humour, tact and patience? If so, come and join our staff. Our large and friendly restaurant requires waiting staff to join our team.

The hours are flexible and we have vacancies for both full and part time staff. The rate of pay is excellent with extra payment for weekend working. We will provide you with a full uniform and if you work after 10.30 pm, transport home will be provided free of charge.

If you are interested in working as part of our team, please contact Joanne Greatorex on 01803 478291. Interviews will be held during the week commencing 2 August.

In return, we expect our staff to be friendly, enthusiastic and helpful. You should be able to deal *communicate* with a wide range of people and be of a clean and smart appearance. Experience is useful but not essential as full training will be given.

Insert this paragraph 40 mm from left margin

Emphasise these words

Exercise 3.12

Recall the document called Exercise 3.12 from the CD-ROM. Make the amendments as shown. Save the document as Hygiene and print one copy. A correct version appears in the worked examples on the CD-ROM.

Recall this document stored under Exercise 3.12. Amend as shown. Use a ragged or a justified right margin. Save as HYGIENE and print one copy.

FOOD HYGIENE ← Centre this heading

Important! Please note the following rules when preparing food in this kitchen.

Inset this paragraph 50 mm from left margin.

Before handling food please ensure that you have washed your hands thoroughly using soap and hot water. Ensure you use the correct chopping board for raw meats and cooked foods. The board for raw meats is made of glass, the wooden board is for breads and the plastic board is for vegetables and cooked meats. It is very important that you use the correct board and ensure it is scrubbed clean after use.

The refrigerator should be kept at a constant temperature in order to ensure that food poisoning organisms are unable to multiply. If you stock the fridge to its capacity you must adjust the temperature to ensure it remains cold. Placing large amounts of food into the fridge will raise the temperature as it has to work extra hard to cool the food.

When storing food in the fridge, remember to place raw meat and fish on the lower shelves away from cooked food. This will help avoid cross contamination. All food must be kept covered, particularly cooked meats and fish.

Stock control should be efficient. Remember to look at the 'best before' dates when storing food and use the oldest first. Do not use foods that are past the 'best before' date. Left-over food should not be kept for longer than a day or two depending on its type.

Please emphasise this sentence

Exercise 3.13

Recall the document called Exercise 3.13 from the CD-ROM. Make the amendments as shown. Save the document as Writing and print one copy. A correct version appears in the worked examples on the CD-ROM.

Recall this document stored under Exercise 3.13. Amend as shown. Use a ragged or justified right margin. Save as WRITING and print one copy.

CREATIVE WRITING

Do you think you have what it takes to write a best-selling novel? Would you like to see your name in print?

Emphasise this sentence

Why not try our creative writing classes and find out if you have hidden talents. Many of our students have become published writers. Some regularly contribute to national magazines and journals, other have become published authors. All have enjoyed the experience of writing for pleasure.

Our classes are held on Wednesday evenings from 7.00pm until 9.00pm. The tutor is Veronica Whitby, an author with many years of successful experience, writing for magazines and newspapers.

She has had several volumes of short stories published and is currently working on her first novel.

Veronica offers expert tuition and carefully considered, constructive criticism of your work. Whether you dream of writing stage plays, film scripts, articles, novels or poetry, the techniques you will learn will be invaluable to your writing.

Come along and try a class — who knows you may be the next J.K. Rowling!

Exercise 3.14

Recall the document called Exercise 3.14 from the CD-ROM. Make the amendments as shown. Save the document as Homes and print one copy. A correct version appears in the worked examples on the CD-ROM.

> Recall this document stored under Exercise 3.14.
> Amend as shown. Adjust the line length to
> 9 cm. Use a justified right margin. Save
> as HOMES and print one copy.

SHOW HOMES

The Ocean Drive property development offers a wide selection of beautifully designed new homes at reasonable prices.

The development is conveniently situated just a 10 minute drive from Sandy Beach. Local schools and hospital are close by making this development ideal for families.

> Inset this paragraph 20 mm from the left margin.

The houses range from one bedroom starter homes to four bedroom deluxe properties. All have their own private parking space and the three and four bedroom properties include a double garage. Many properties have wonderful views across open countryside to the sea.

The houses are ready for inspection now. The show home is open seven days a week. If you are able to exchange contracts within the next three weeks you will have the opportunity to choose your own kitchen and bathroom fittings.

Prices start from as little as £120,000. Phoenix Properties are also able to offer great part-exchange deals. This means we will purchase your existing property, subject to terms and conditions.

Exercise 3.15

Recall the document called Exercise 3.15 from the CD-ROM. Make the amendments as shown. Save the document as Dig and print one copy. A correct version appears in the worked examples on the CD-ROM.

Recall this document stored under Exercise 3.15. Amend as shown. Use a ragged or justified right margin. Save as Dig and print one copy.

ARCHAEOLOGICAL DIG ← *Centre this heading*

As some of you are aware, the Phoenix Staff Association has decided to hold an archaeological dig on the waste ground at the rear of the sports field.

This will take place on Saturday and Sunday, 9 and 10 August. We will be starting at 7.30 am and continuing until dusk each day.

Inset this paragraph 30 mm from left margin

It is hoped that we will find many items of interest. As the head office building is on the site of a former pottery we are sure we will find lots of interesting cups and saucers if nothing else!

Do come along and join in. We will have a team of experts on hand to advise us. These include Dr John Clarke, a well-known local historian and archaeologist Dr Kathy McIntyre.

Family and friends are most welcome. Refreshments will be provided throughout the day.

Exercise 3.16

Recall the document called Exercise 3.16 from the CD-ROM. Make the amendments as shown. Save the document as Catering and print one copy. A correct version appears in the worked examples on the CD-ROM.

Recall this document stored under Exercise 3.16. Amend as shown. Use a ragged or justified right margin. Save as CATERING and print one copy.

FOOD ORDERING SERVICE ← Centre this heading

If you are too busy to prepare meals but want to eat home-cooked food then call us. We will provide ready-cooked meals to your door. All you need to do is choose from our extensive menu and give us a ring. The meals will arrive ready for you to heat in your own oven or microwave.

extensive   *Casseroles and roasts*

Our menu is ~~wide~~, ranging from fresh pasta dishes to more traditional ~~stews and soups~~. Desserts are a real speciality of ours. If you have a particular preference for a dish then talk to us. If you are able to give us some advance notice then we are happy to cook meals to order.

We also cater for dinner parties. Ask for our special dinner party menus. These cater for four to twelve people. Vegetarian dinner party menus are also available.

If you are hosting a large party or wedding talk to us about your requirements. We can provide everything you need from buffets to formal dinners.

Inset this paragraph 30 mm from left margin

Please emphasise this sentence

Exercise 3.17

Recall the document called Exercise 3.17 from the CD-ROM. Make the amendments as shown. Save the document as Homeopathy and print one copy. A correct version appears in the worked examples on the CD-ROM.

Recall this document stored under Exercise 3.17
Amend as shown. Adjust the line length to
10 cm and use a justified right margin.
Save as Homeopathy and print one copy.

Homeopathy ← 'Emphasise this heading

This 'alternative' form of medicine is now very popular.
It has been around since the end of the nineteenth
Century.

The treatments used are completely natural. They are derived from animal, mineral and plant substances. They are safe to use and have no side-effects. The dose given is highly diluted as this has been found to be more effective.

The symptoms are treated as part of a larger condition and the selected remedy will be ~~used~~ given to treat the condition as a whole. The remedy will be selected on its ability to start the same symptoms in a healthy person.

Although you can buy remedies at chemists it is much
better if you consult a qualified homeopath. Some
General Practitioners now offer this service. You
will be able to find a local homeopath listed
in your telephone directory.

Three column table

In this section you will learn about:

- creating a table
- moving columns and rows
- tidying up the table
- removing grid lines

One of the documents you will be expected to produce in the examination is a three column table. Look at Figure 3.5 below:

NAME	PAYROLL NUMBER	BRANCH
Mark Johnson	1920	Peterborough
Florence Sheppard	1431	Exeter
Tanya Bartlett	1377	Manchester
Emma Kolenko	1548	Hull
Ian Carter	1632	Bristol
Derek Fisher	1844	Bradford
Henrietta Golder	1673	Peterborough
Laura North	1397	Hull
Adam Elliott	1107	Bradford

Figure 3.5 Three column table

This column has been set up using the table editor facilities.

Exercise 3.18

Create a three column table with ten rows.

Method

1   Go to the **Table** icon on the toolbar ▦ . Click on the icon and the following grid will appear (Figure 3.6):

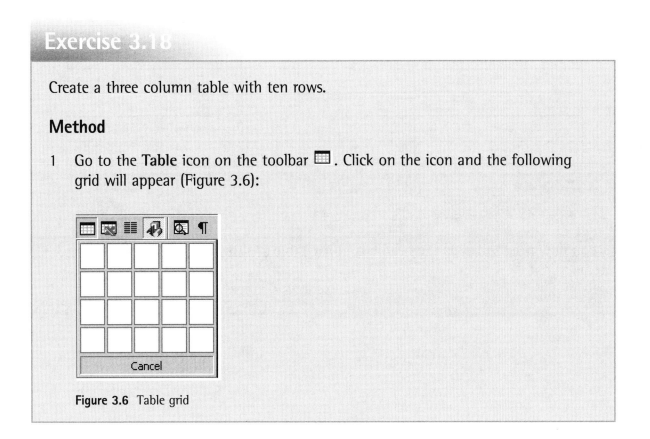

Figure 3.6 Table grid

2   Click on the top left-hand square and drag out the number of columns and down for the number of rows that you will require in your table. For this exercise you will require three columns and ten rows. The table grid will change colour and the dimensions of your table will be given at the bottom of the grid. You must keep holding down the mouse button whilst you are doing this (see Figure 3.7 below). To calculate the number of columns and rows you require, just count the number of columns across and then the number of lines down.

Figure 3.7 The table grid showing a 10 × 3 table

3   Once you are sure you have a correctly sized grid, then release the mouse button. The grid will now appear in your document as shown in Figure 3.8 below.

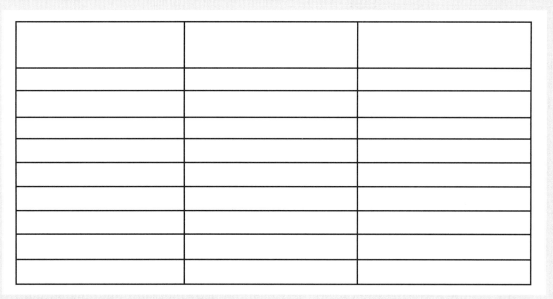

Figure 3.8 Table grid

You now need to key in the headings of the table as shown above (Figure 3.5).

Exercise 3.19

Enter the table headings into the grid.

Method

1   Click in the top left-hand cell of your table and key in the word 'Name'.
2   Press the **tab** key once to move to the next cell. Key in the words 'Payroll Number'.
3   Press the **tab** key once to move to the next cell. Key in the word 'Branch'.
4   In order to leave a space between the heading and the text of the table, press the **return** key (whilst still in the third column). Emphasise the headings using the usual methods. The headings are now complete. The table should look like Figure 3.9 below.

NAME	PAYROLL NUMBER	BRANCH

Figure 3.9 Table with column headings

Key in the table text.

Method

1   Key in the text as shown above (Figure 3.5), using the methods shown. The table should now look like Figure 3.10 below.

NAME	PAYROLL NUMBER	BRANCH
Mark Johnson	1920	Peterborough
Florence Sheppard	1431	Exeter
Tanya Bartlett	1377	Manchester
Emma Kolenko	1548	Hull
Ian Carter	1632	Bristol
Derek Fisher	1844	Bradford
Henrietta Golder	1673	Peterborough
Laura North	1397	Hull
Adam Elliott	1107	Bradford

Figure 3.10 Table with text

Moving columns and rows

You will find an instruction to change the order of the columns. You can, of course, make this amendment as you are keying in the text. However, you may find it easier and more accurate if you key in the text exactly as shown and then move the table around using the table editor facilities.

Move the 'Payroll' column so that it becomes the last column of the table. You will need to move the entire column, including the heading, so that it becomes the final column.

Method

1   Highlight the column you wish to move, in this case the 'Payroll' column. You can highlight a column by moving the cursor to the top of the column until it turns into a solid black arrow. When you can see the black arrow, click the mouse button so that the entire column is highlighted (see Figure 3.11 below).

NAME	PAYROLL NUMBER	BRANCH
Mark Johnson	1920	Peterborough
Florence Sheppard	1431	Exeter
Tanya Bartlett	1377	Manchester
Emma Kolenko	1548	Hull
Ian Carter	1632	Bristol
Derek Fisher	1844	Bradford
Henrietta Golder	1673	Peterborough
Laura North	1397	Hull
Adam Elliott	1107	Bradford

Figure 3.11 Table with column highlighted

2 Make sure the cursor is still in the highlighted column. Now click the mouse button and hold it down, the cursor will change appearance. Move the cursor to the end of the final (Branch) column and let go. The columns will have moved.

Note: you may need to practise this a few times until you get it right. If the columns do not end up in the correct place, remember to click on **Undo** to get the table back to where you started.

Tidying up the table

If any of the lines have moved out of place and have split lines so that the words have wrapped down to the next line, you should tidy up the table so that it looks neat.

Exercise 3.22

Ensure that all the text remains on a single line.

Method

1 Using the mouse, drag the cursor over the vertical gridlines between the columns. The cursor will change to a double arrow cursor with a space between the two arrows. Position the space of these arrows over the gridline so that it fits exactly.
2 Now drag the column out to the right. The word(s) that have been pushed down to a second line should jump back up once the column is wide enough. When it is a suitable size, let go.
3 Repeat this for each column as necessary. Remember that once you have altered one column it often pushes the others out of line – be patient!

Removing the grid lines

The gridlines, that is the black border lines of the table, *must not* be printed in the examination. These are quite simple to remove.

Exercise 3.23

Remove all gridlines from the table.

Method

1   Select the entire table, by clicking on the top of the table and dragging the mouse from left to right. The entire table should now be highlighted.

2   Go to the **Border** icon on the toolbar ⊞ and click on the drop down menu. The following options will appear on screen (Figure 3.12):

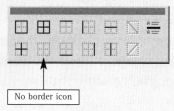

No border icon

Figure 3.12 Border options

3   Choose the **No border** icon as shown in Figure 3.12. The gridlines should now be removed and your table will look like Figure 3.13 below.

NAME	PAYROLL NUMBER	BRANCH
Mark Johnson	1920	Peterborough
Florence Sheppard	1431	Exeter
Tanya Bartlett	1377	Manchester
Emma Kolenko	1548	Hull
Ian Carter	1632	Bristol
Derek Fisher	1844	Bradford
Henrietta Golder	1673	Peterborough
Laura North	1397	Hull
Adam Elliott	1107	Bradford

Figure 3.13 Completed table

It has probably taken you quite some time to work through this table using the methods given above. It is a very accurate method to ensure that the text remains in the same columns and, with a little practice, will become much quicker once you are used to moving lines around and entering text into the table editor.

Exercise 3.24

Key in the following table. Amend as shown. Save as Exercise 3.24 and print one copy. A correct version appears in the worked examples on the CD-ROM.

Toy	Price	Age Range
Soft play mat	£19.99	0 - 2 years
Science kit	£29.99	10 - 15 years
Dolls' house	£75.00	5 - 10 years
Baking set	£12.99	6 - 12 years
Garage	£35.00	5 - 9 years
Snakes and ladders game	£10.00	4 - adult
Craft set	£15.00	6 - adult
Yacht	£20.00	6 - adult
Mermaid dressing-up kit	£35.00	4 - 6 years
Baby doll	£25.00	3 - 10 years
Remote control car	£70.00	10 years - adult
Ludo	£10.00	5 years - adult
Teddy bear	£20.00	3 years plus
Cot mobile	£35.00	0 - 2 years

Display the Age Range column before the Price column eg Toy Age Range Price

Exercise 3.25

Key in the following table. Amend as shown. Save as Exercise 3.25 and print one copy. A correct version appears in the worked examples on the CD-ROM.

Products	Price	Skin Type
Day time moisturiser	£5.00	Normal
Night time moisturiser	£9.00	Greasy
Light day cream	£6.00	Combination
Hand cream	£4.00	All
Cleansing lotion	£4.00	Greasy
Toner	£5.00	Greasy
Day time moisturiser	£8.00	Dry
Night moisturiser	£9.00	Dry
Eye cream	£7.00	Dry
Fine wrinkle cream	£9.00	Combination
Body lotion	£6.00	All
Foot cream	£4.00	All
Concealer	£5.00	Greasy

Display the Skin Type column before the Price column

eg

Products	Skin Type	Price
Day time moisturiser	Normal	£5.00

Exercise 3.26

Key in the following table. Amend as shown. Save as Exercise 3.26 and print one copy. A correct version appears in the worked examples on the CD-ROM.

SHRUB	TYPE	FLOWERS
Ceanothus	Evergreen	May – June
Abelia	Deciduous	June – September
Periwinkle	Evergreen	April – September
Star jasmine	Evergreen	July – August
Lilac	Deciduous	May – June
Spiraea	Deciduous	June – September
Elder	Deciduous	May – July
Rosemary	Evergreen	April – May
Honeysuckle	Semi-evergreen	May – June
Tree mallow	Semi – evergreen	July – September
Kalmia	Evergreen	April – June
Indigo bush	Deciduous	July – September
Lacebark	Semi – evergreen	June – September
Hebe	Evergreen	May – November

Display the FLOWERS column before the TYPE column

ie

SHRUB	FLOWERS	TYPE
Ceanothus	May – June	Evergreen

Exercise 3.27

Recall the document stored under Exercise 3.27. Key in the three column table and amend as shown. Save as Beauty and print one copy. A correct version appears in the worked examples on the CD-ROM.

> Recall this document stored under Exercise 3.27. Amend as shown. Use a ragged or justified right margin. Save as Beauty and print one copy. Do not rule the table.

BEAUTY TREATMENTS

This month Phoenix Beauty is offering amazing deals on some of their most popular treatments. We anticipate demand to be high, so it is advisable to book in advance.

TREATMENT	OFFER PRICE	STAFF
Full leg wax	£8	Sabrina
Half leg wax	£4	Sabrina
Eyelash tint	£8	Laura
Eyebrow tint	£10	Laura
Manicure	£12	Peter
Pedicure	£10	Peter
Facial	£12	Candice
Hair restyle	£40	Max
Highlights	£60	Jon

Display the NORMAL PRICE column before the OFFER PRICE column.
Eg
TREATMENT	STAFF	OFFER PRICE
Full leg wax	Sabrina	£8

When booking, please ask for the member of staff shown above.

Hurry, these offers are only available until the end of August.

Exercise 3.28

Recall the document stored under Exercise 3.28. Key in the three column table and amend as shown. Save as Deals and print one copy. A correct version appears in the worked examples on the CD-ROM.

> Recall this document stored under Exercise 3.28. Amend as shown. Use a ragged or justified margin. Save as Deals and print one copy. Do not rule the table.

LAST MINUTE DEALS

We still have some last minute availability on holidays due to start in the next few weeks. Prices have been cut by up to 50%.

The price shown includes airport taxes and transfer fees.

DESTINATION	PRICE PER PERSON	HOTEL
Paris	£250	Grande
London	£140	Windsor
Malta	£425	Cornucopia
Cyprus	£395	Elysium
Tuscany	£550	Cellai
Vienna	£325	Atlantis
Rome	£189	Edera
Athens	£275	Viminale
Madrid	£300	Grand Harbour
Florida	£650	Surfside
Boston	£750	Seaport
Las Vegas	£530	Excalibur
Amsterdam	£220	Tulip
Copenhagen	£265	Phoenix

> Display the HOTEL column before the PRICE PER PERSON column.
>
> Eg DESTINATION HOTEL PRICE PER PERSON
>   Paris   Grande £250

If you would like further information regarding any of these special offers, please contact us.

Exercise 3.29

Recall the document stored under Exercise 3.29 Key in the three column table and amend as shown. Save as Stationery and print one copy. A correct version appears in the worked examples on the CD-ROM.

Recall this document stored under Ex 3.29 , Amend as shown. Use a ragged or justified right margin. Save as Stationery and print one copy. Do not rule the table.

STATIONERY REQUESTS

Unfortunately staff have been taking far too much stationery from the stockroom without permission during the past few months. This has cost the company a considerable amount of money.

As from Monday staff may only collect stationery on Wednesday mornings between 10 am and 12 noon. If stationery is required urgently at other times, then a request should be made directly to Mike Ayers or Judy Potter.

The following items can be ordered without authorisation from a senior staff member.

ITEM	CODE	QUANTITY
CS envelopes (25)	CENV	1
DL envelopes (50)	DLEN	1
A4 paper (ream)	ALAP	1
AS paper (ream)	ASAP	1
A3 paper (ream)	AEAP	1
Black ballpoint pen	BBEP	5
Pencil	HBBI	5
Eraser	ERAS	1
Pencil sharpener	PSHP	1
Ruler	RRUL	1
Staples (500 box)	SPAL	1
Correction pen	CPEN	2

Display QUANTITY column before the CODE column
eg ITEM   QUANTITY   CODE
CS envelopes   1   CENV

If you require an item that is not listed above, or a larger quantity than shown, please speak to your line manager.

Consolidation practice

The following consolidation exercises will help you prepare for the Word Processing examination. Try to complete each set of consolidation pieces in the usual time allowed for this exam, that is 1 hour and 30 minutes.

Remember to check your work carefully, and correct any errors before printing. You should print one copy of each document. The correct versions of these exercises can be found in the worked examples on the CD-ROM.

Consolidation 1 – Document 1

> Recall this document stored under Antique Article. Amend as shown. Change to double linespacing (except where indicated). Adjust the line length to 14 cm. Use a justified right margin. Save as Antiques and print one copy.

BUYING AT AUCTION

Buying items at auction can be nerve-wracking, exciting and fun. Your *local* newspaper will give details of forthcoming sales and you can go along and view the items for sale. Alternatively you can ask for a catalogue to be sent to you, although there will probably be a charge for this service. *It is however important to examine any items that have caught your interest as once you have made a successful bid you are legally bound to purchase the item.*

On the day of the sale, there will be opportunities for viewing the goods ~~for the last time~~. Once you have decided that you wish to purchase an item, you have three options.

You can attend the sale and bid yourself, you can place your bids by telephone or you can leave your bid with the auctioneer.

Move to point marked Ⓐ.

When the bidding is complete the auctioneer will signal this by banging the gavel, which is a small hammer, on the rostrum. The name of the successful bidder will then be recorded.

Once the gavel has fallen, the buyer is legally bound to complete the transaction. A deposit payment must be made immediately with the balance paid before the goods are taken away. You are usually given just a few days to organise this.

Emphasise this sentence

This paragraph only in single linespacing

The goods are sold in lots, each with a number. When the sale starts, the auctioneer will tell you which lot is being sold. The auctioneer will suggest a figure to begin the bidding. This is usually just below the lowest estimate.

If people are interested in buying the lot then they will signal their interest to the auctioneer. This can be done by nodding, waving or holding up a number given out by the auction house. The bidding goes up in increments. The amount of each increment will depend on the value of the item being sold.

(A) are

buying

If you interested in ~~starting a collection of~~ antiques then ~~attending~~ visiting (/) auctions and sale rooms may prove to be enormous fun. You will learn a great deal about your particular interest and you may find a bargain.

Document 2

Recall this document stored under Antique Display. Amend as shown. Use a ragged or justified right hand margin. Save as Auction Display and print one copy.

SELLING AT AUCTION ← Centre this heading

If you have some items that you no longer want, a good way to sell them is at auction. You may be surprised at the amount of money others will pay for goods you have finished with.

If you are able to take your goods to the auction house, then do so. The receptionist will be able to help you to find the valuer who specialises in the items you are selling. They will examine your goods and give you their valuation.

Insert this paragraph 50 mm from the left margin

The valuer will give you an estimate as to the lowest and highest figures your goods might expect to make. He or she may also ask you about the provenance, or history of the item. Do not be afraid to tell them anything you know about the item, even if you think it is insignificant. The information will help the valuer build up a picture of the item and can help make a correct identification and valuation.

You will have to pay commission on the sale of your goods. This is usually around 15% plus VAT. However, if your goods realise a much higher figure than you expected it is well worth selling items in this way.

A reserve figure will also be mentioned. A reserve figure is one that the goods must reach in order to be sold. This cuts the risk of selling at auction as you can set the reserve figure to ensure you do not sell the goods for much less than they are worth.

Document 3

Recall this document stored under Antique Table. Amend as shown. Use a ragged or justified right margin. Save as Auction Table and print one copy. Do not rule the table.

Notice to Staff - Forthcoming Auction

Our next auction of general household goods will be held on Saturday 23 March at 2.00 pm at the Phoenix Auction House. The items will be available to view from 10.00 am on the day of the sale.

Given below is a list of the lots that have been received. We are expecting many more items before the final entry date for the sale. A catalogue will be produced shortly after that date. The name of the vendor has been included in this list for recording purposes. These will not appear in the catalogue.

Display the Item column before the Lot Number column
eg   Name   Lot Number
Jon Van Housen   marble washstand   469

NAME	LOT NUMBER	ITEM
Jon Van Housen	469	Marble washstand
Gordon Briggs	521	Medicine box
Megenta Cummings	178	Georgian silver teapot
Emma Westlake	129	Art deco vase
Dan Goldblum	335	Rural landscape painting
Paul Amers	267	Grandfather clock
Callum Finlay	242	Oak dining table
Razia Shamid	193	Victorian pine dresser
Polly Chisham	483	Edwardian display cabinet
Grace Ivan	351	Wedgwood dinner service
Laverne Killock	422	Art deco teapot
Nancy Plummer	376	Victorian chest of drawers
Olivia Quinten	320	Mahogany dining table

The quality of these items is high and we are expecting the sale to do well. As a reminder, our specialist ceramic sale will be held during the first week of May. We have already received a great deal of interest in this, from both buyers and sellers.

Consolidation 2 – Document 1

Recall this document stored under Jewellery Article. Amend as shown. Change to double linespacing (except where indicated). Adjust the line length to 14 cm and use a justified right margin. Save as Jewellery 1 and print one copy.

DIAMONDS ← Centre this heading

If you are thinking of buying some pieces of diamond jewellery then there are a number of points that need consideration. A large diamond is not necessarily the best. A variety of factors will be used to determine the value of the stone. These factors are known as the 4 Cs – Cut, colour, clarity and carat.

Colour Unfortunately, these are very rare.

The colour of the diamond will significantly affect its value. The rarest diamonds have no colour at all. The colour scale ranges from D to Z. Colourless diamonds are rated D, those that are light yellow are rated Z.

Emphasise this sentence

It can however, be very difficult to detect the difference between the colours especially when it has been mounted as jewellery.

As a guide, diamonds that have a J colour grade, usually have a yellow shading that can be detected by the naked eye.

Move this section to →

Cut

The cut will have the greatest impact on the appearance of the diamond. It is essential that any diamond you buy has been well cut. It is this that will give the diamond its fire and brilliance.

Document 1 (cont)

With respect to its width

A diamond that has been cut too shallow/will allow too much light to pass through the diamond, leaving little light to reflect.

This will mean the diamond is dull and lacking in sparkle.

too much

One that has been cut too deeply will allow/light to escape from the sides of the stone, also making it appear dull.

Clarity

imperfections ✓

The clarity of the diamond refers to the tiny ~~flaws~~ that naturally occur on the stones. A flawless diamond has a much greater value than one with inclusions, which is the term for the tiny imperfections.

The inclusions are classified on a scale. This ranges from WS1, which has very few inclusions through to I3 which has a number of inclusions. These inclusions are easily visible to the naked eye.

This section only in single linespacing

Carat

used   term

~~Using~~ the term carat/to describe diamonds is different to the ~~carat~~ used for describing gold. A carat is a unit of measurement which the jewellery industry uses to weigh diamonds. The more the diamond weighs the more the diamond will cost.   As a general rule,

However, remember that size isn't everything. A valuer will also take into account the cut, clarity and colour of a stone when making a judgement.

Document 2

Recall this document stored under Jewellery Display. Amend as shown. Use a ragged or justified right hand margin. Save as Jewellery2 and print one copy.

BIRMINGHAM JEWELLERY QUARTER

The Birmingham Jellewery Quarter has been home to some of the worlds most highly skilled goldsmiths and jewellery makers for over 200 years. During its peak, over 60,000 people were employed in the precious metal and associated trades.

The Jewellery Quarter is an area that has been associated with these trades since the late eighteenth century. Many tradesmen worked either from home or small workshops, specialising in a particular craft.

These crafts often complemented each other and this led to a sense of community in the area. The strength of the community fostered a national and international respect for the Jewellery Quarter.

Inset this paragraph 40 mm from the left margin

For over two hundred years the Jewellery Quarter was a trade and manufacturing area. The first shops were opened in the district in the 1970s. It is now a well known area for both the trade and the public to browse and enjoy.

By 1861 over 7,000 people were employed in the jewellery trade. As trade flourished, so did the area. New streets containing large residential properties were developed, together with a number of small terraces for the tradesmen.

Document 3

Recall this document stored under Jewellery Table. Amend as shown. Use a ragged or justified right margin. Save as Jewellery3 and print one copy. Do not rule the table.

JEWELLERY SALE

We are currently clearing our stocks to make way for some exciting new ranges. These are due in store in June. The following items have limited availability and once sold, we will not be able to order more supplies.

All items have 18 carat gold mountings and are made to the highest standard.

Display the SALE PRICE column before the STYLE column eg

ITEM	STYLE	SALE PRICE
Diamond brooch	Modern	£300

ITEM	SALE PRICE	STYLE
Solitaire diamond ring	£750	Modern
Diamond earrings	£250	Modern
Sapphire necklace	£500	Traditional
Emerald ring	£650	Antique
Amethyst ring	£150	Antique
Opal bracelet	£180	Traditional
Diamond pendant	£350	Modern
Emerald necklace	£550	Antique
Ruby ring	£350	Traditional
Diamond bracelet	£400	Modern
Emerald earrings	£250	Antique

We are also offering a range of matching wedding and engagement rings at clearance prices.

Full details of these pieces, including photographs, can be found on our website www.phoenixjewels.com.

Consolidation 3 – Document 1

Recall this document stored under Fireworks. Amend as shown. Use double linespacing (except where indicated). Adjust the line length to 13 cm and use a justified right margin. Save as DISPLAY NOTES and print one copy.

Hosting A Firework Display ← *Centre this heading*

These notes are intended to help you organise a firework ~~show~~ *display* ✓ that is safe and enjoyable. Running a display takes a lot of work so try to share the load by planning ahead. You will need to ensure that you have enough helpers who each have a particular responsibility. ~~They must all be trained in first aid.~~

Move to point marked ■

Further information on positioning the fireworks can be found on the firework safety website.

You must inform the authorities that you are planning a display. These include the fire brigade, |police, local authority| and local first aid groups such as St John's Ambulance. This should be one of your first tasks.

This paragraph in Single linespacing

The space required for your display is very important. You must ensure that you have at least 50 m x 20 m for your firing area. Beyond this you will need a dropping zone for spent fireworks of 100 m x 50 m in the downward direction.

Such as overhead Cables

Spectators should be kept back on the opposite site from the dropping zone at least 25 m from the firing zone.

The area should be clear and free from obstructions such as |buildings, trees| and hazards. There should be as many safe entrances and exits as possible. These must be away from the firing and dropping zones.

Document 1 (cont)

Insert this paragraph 10mm from left margin

and exits

Ensure that all entrances / are well-lit, clearly signposted and free from obstruction. Clear away any undergrowth or long grass. Check that animals are not housed nearby. It is most important that you ensure you can cater for disabled spectators safely.

Have plenty of metal litter bins around the site.

Car parking is always something that needs careful consideration. As falling fireworks can cause damage it is important that designated car parking is kept well away from the display area. It should also be upwind of the display and clear of the dropping zone. The car parking entrance should be separate to the pedestrian entrance. *Signpost the car park clearly.*

essential

Crowd control is ~~a must~~ and needs careful planning. You will need to have one steward for every 250 spectators. Make sure that the stewards are easily identifiable.

They will need to be trained in emergency procedures and have practised safety drills. If you are expecting a very large crowd then do contact the Police. They will be able to give you advice on how to deal with crowds.

Document 2

Recall this document stored under Phoenix. Amend as shown. Use a ragged or justified right margin. Save as DISPLAY2 and print one copy.

PHOENIX FIREWORK DISPLAY ← Centre this heading

The Phoenix Enterprises Staff Association will be holding their annual firework display at Phoenix Recreation Ground on Saturday 7 November. The gates are open from 6.30 pm and the fun and fireworks start at 7.15 pm.

After the fireworks there will be music provided by a local swing band. Hot food will be available and the club bar will be opening from 6.30 pm until midnight.

The display of fireworks will be our largest so far with the show taking approximately 35 minutes.

These very special fireworks will be digitally controlled to ensure that the timing is absolutely perfect.

Tickets are available from Mandy Jerome, the Club Secretary at a cost of £2 for adults and £1 for children under 14 years. Non-members are welcome to attend this event. Tickets are limited and will be issued on a first-come, first-served basis

Car parking will be provided at the Staff Association Sports Centre. A small charge will be made for non-members. Further parking will be available at the Redwood site.

Document 3

Recall this document stored under Events. Amend as shown. Use a ragged or justified right margin. Save as DISPLAY 3 and print one copy. Do not rule the table.

PHOENIX ENTERPRISES STAFF ASSOCIATION

This year we have organised a number of events for our members. We have tried to ensure that the activities will appeal to all ages and tastes.

Our theatre nights have been very popular and these are held on Monday evenings. A full programme of shows can be found on the Staff Association Noticeboard.

For further information or to book tickets, please contact Mandy Jerome, the club secretary on extension 232. Please note that prices include coach travel where appropriate.

MONTH	EVENT	NON-MEMBER PRICE
December	Shopping trip to Calais	£35
February	Skiing Weekend in Scotland	£220
March	Day trip to London	£20
June	Weekend in St Ives	£150
August	Treasure hunt	£7
July	Garden show	£4
October	Pub quiz night	£4
June	Wimbledon visit	£60
May	Hot air ballooning	£100
All year	Theatre trips	£12
September	Trip to the Eden Project	£30
October	Alton Towers Visit	£25
November	Ice skating day	£20
April	Hampton Court day trip	£25
January	Weekend in Bath	£170

Display the EVENT column before NON MEMBER PRICE column eg

EVENT   MONTH   NON MEMBER PRICE
Shopping trip   December   £35
to Calais

Membership of the Staff Association costs £20 per family per year. Benefits include discounted tickets for events and free use of the sports and social club.

Taking the examination

This section tells you exactly what the examiner will be looking for when marking your work. It does this by showing you the most common errors in documents submitted for the examination, together with hints on how to resolve these errors.

It also includes three examination practice exercises for you to complete to prepare you for the OCR examination.

Document 1

This task requires you to recall an existing document, usually an article or report, and make the necessary amendments. You may be asked to change line spacing, adjust the line length, use a specified text alignment and inset a paragraph from the margin. You will also be expected to number continuation pages.

Look at Figures 3.14 and 3.15 below. The first document is correct, the second has five errors. Can you spot them?

FINDING AN ESTATE AGENT

Choosing the right estate agent for you is much more important than you might think. It is essential that if you are to get your early sale at the right price then you find one who is experienced with the type of property you are selling.

You should talk to at least three different estate agencies. Look at the advertisements in their windows and local newspapers. Make sure that the properties they are advertising are similar in price and type to the one you are hoping to sell.

If you own a one bedroomed flat in a residential estate, then there is no point employing an estate agent that deals in luxury detached houses in exclusive estates.

Remember that you both want the same thing - a quick and trouble-free sale. Ask if they have recently sold any properties on their books that are similar to yours. If so, discuss with them the speed at which these properties sold and the approximate price each has fetched.

Have a look around the area in which your property is situated. Make a note of the number of For Sale boards. Check to see which of the agents have the most properties for sale. This will give you an idea of the estate agent's popularity.

Figure 3.14 Correct version

FINDING AN ESTATE AGENT

Choosing the right estate agent for you is much more important than you might think. It is essential that if you are to get your early sale at the right price then you find one who is experienced with the type of property you are selling.

Have a look around the area in which your property is situated. Make a note of the number of For Sale boards. Check to see which of the agents have the most properties for sale. This will give you an idea of the estate agent's popularity

You should talk to at least three different estate agencies. Look at the advertisements in their windows and local newspapers. Make sure that the properties they are advertising are similar in price and type to the one you are hoping to sell. If you own a one bedroomed flat in a residential estate, then there is no point employing an estate agent that deals in luxury detached houses in exclusive estates.

Remember that you both want the same thing - a quick and trouble-free sale. Ask if they have recently sold any properties on their books that are similar to yours. If so, discuss with them the speed at which these properties sold and the approximate price each has fetched.

Figure 3.15 Incorrect version

Error 1
The line length has not been adjusted.

Solution
Remember to alter the line length. The size of the line length will be contained in the instruction box at the top of the page. You may wish to highlight the instructions in this box as quite a number are placed here.

If you have an uneven line length then maybe you have just pulled in the margins using the ruler bar at the top of the page. This method is not reliable if you are moving text around. Follow the instructions given on page 99.

Error 2

The text is not justified.

Solution

The instructions for justifying text can be found on page 21. Again, the instruction for this will be in the large box at the top of the page. Remember to tick off the amendments as you make them.

Error 3

The paragraph beginning 'Remember, you both ...' has not been changed to single line spacing.

Solution

Instructions for changing line spacing can be found on page 9. Don't forget to proofread your work carefully to ensure that all amendments have been made. It can be difficult to follow all the amendments, particularly if you move around the page. Try to follow the amendments logically. Start at the top and work down. If you have to make amendments to a paragraph that is going to be moved, make them *before* you move it. That way you will not become distracted.

Error 4

The paragraph of text beginning 'Have a look around ...' has been moved incorrectly.

Solution

Be very careful when moving or copying text. Once you have made the move, read the instructions again to ensure you have done so correctly. This is a very common error.

Error 5

The heading has not been centred.

Solution

Again, this comes down to careful proofreading. Highlight the amendments and work logically down the page. Check your work very carefully to ensure that all amendments have been made before you print your work. If you are adjusting the line length, make sure you do this before you make any other amendments. This will help to ensure that amendments such as centring a heading will be correct, as if you centre first then change the line length, you may find the heading is no longer centred.

Document 2

Look at Figures 3.16 and 3.17 below. The first document is correct, the second has three errors. Can you spot them?

FOOTBALL FIVE-A-SIDE KNOCKOUT COMPETITION

The Student's Union have organised a five-a-side football knockout competition. This will take place on <u>Saturday 18 October</u> at the Sports Hall.

The competition starts at 10.30 am and it is anticipated that the finals will kick off at 4.00 pm.

> The competition is open to anyone. Registration forms can be collected from Louis Carpenter, in the Student Union Office. An entry fee of £2.50 is payable for each team. All team players must be over 16 years of age.

The Student Refectory will be open on the day for refreshments and snacks.

Figure 3.16 Correct version

FOOTBALL FIVE-A-SIDE KNOCKOUT COMPETITION

The Student's Union have organised a five-a-side football knockout competition. This will take place on <u>Saturday 18 October at the Sports Hall</u>.

The competition starts at 10.30 am and it is anticipated that the finals will kick off at 4.00 pm.

The competition is open to anyone. Registration forms can be collected from Louis Carpenter, in the Student Union Office. An entry fee of £2.50 is payable for each team. All team players must be over 16 years of age.

The Student Refectory will be open on the day for refreshments and snacks.

Figure 3.17 Incorrect version

Error 1
The heading has not been emphasised.

Solution
Careful proofreading will solve these types of problems. Information on how to emphasise text can be found on page 55.

Error 2

The paragraph starting 'The competition is open' has not been inset.

Solution

You must ensure that you make all the amendments given on the examination paper. In order to do this, tick off each amendment as you make it. Once you think you have finished, go back over the paper, reading it carefully to ensure you have not missed any instructions. If you do not know how to inset text, see page 101 for further information.

Error 3

The underlining continues onto other words.

Solution

This is a very common error. You should check the screen, and if you have time and your centre allows, check your printed copy. It can be that when you are moving text, or adding line spaces etc., the turn off underscore code is erased. If you are making this kind of amendment, go back and check that enhancements such as emboldening, line spacing, insetting etc. are as they should be.

Document 3

It is so easy to make errors on the table that you must allow sufficient time to proofread this document very carefully. You are expected to key in a table and rearrange the details including moving a column.

Look at Figures 3.18 and 3.19. Figure 3.18 is correct, Figure 3.19 has three errors. Can you spot them?

SHRUB	FLOWERING SEASON	COLOUR
Callistemon	June-July	Pink
Convolvulus	May-August	White
Forsythia	March-April	Yellow
Hibiscus	July-September	Blue
Indigoferea	July-September	Pink
Kerria	April-May	Yellow
Lavandula	July-September	Lilac
Mahonia	January-May	Yellow
Ozothamnus	June-August	White

Figure 3.18 Correct version

SHRUB	COLOUR	FLOWERING SEASON
Callistemon	Pink	June-July
Convolvulus	White	May-August
Forsythia	Yellow	March-April
Hibiscus	Blue	July-September
Indigoferea	Pink	July-September
Kerria	Yellow	April-May
Lavandula	Lilac	July-September
Mahonia	Yellow	January-May
Ozothamnus	White	June-August

Figure 3.19 Incorrect version

Error 1
There is no space after the headings.

Solution
This is a very common error. You must ensure that you leave a clear line space after the headings of a table. To find out how to do this, look at page 127.

Error 2
The columns 'colour' and 'flowering season' are in the wrong order.

Solution

You must check very carefully where you are placing the new columns when moving them. It is much better to follow the instructions given on page 128 than trying to work out where to put the columns before you start keying in.

Error 3

The gridlines can still be seen.

Solution

Highlight the instruction 'Do not rule the table' so that you do not forget to remove the gridlines. To find out how to remove the grid, look at the instructions on page 130. Do not attempt to key in the table without the lines as it becomes very complicated when moving columns or adjusting space.

Examination practice

To help you prepare for the examination, three full examination papers follow. Try to complete these in exam conditions. That is, finish in the 1 hour and 30 minutes allowed, including printing. Do not ask for help or refer to this book for information on how to do things. Try not to talk to anyone whilst working on these tasks. If you can do all of these then your work will give you a good indication of whether you are ready to sit the real exam. Once you have completed the tasks, you can check your documents with the worked examples on the CD-ROM.

When you are working through these exercises you will need to remember the following:

- If you are unsure of a spelling, use a dictionary as well as the spellchecker.
- Remember to spellcheck your work after you have finished each document.
- Consistency is very important. Make sure that all your work, including spacing between paragraphs, numbers etc., shows a consistent display.
- Continuation sheets must be numbered.
- Ensure that any vertical space you allocate is correct by measuring with a ruler.
- Make sure that you make all the amendments in a document. It can be helpful to tick these off as you go along.
- When checking details from one document to another, you must ensure the details you key in are absolutely correct.
- Once you have finished keying in the text for a document, check with the exam paper that you have not keyed in the same word or line twice, or that you have missed a word or line. These are very common errors and can lose you a large number of marks.

If you can complete all the work within the time without too many errors, then you should now try working on some old examination papers. These will give you a feel for the type of examination paper you are likely to face. You must not become too complacent, even if you are consistently doing well in practice papers, as the examination can make you nervous and this is when it is easy to make mistakes.

The key to success in the examination is proofreading your work carefully, referring back to the examination paper to check that you have keyed in the correct words, not the ones you think are there or should be there!

Examination practice 1 – Document 1

Recall this document stored under Dog Article. Amend as shown. Change to double linespacing (except where indicated). Adjust the line length to 12 cm. Use a justified right margin. Save as Dogs 1 and print one copy.

DOGS

Dogs have been faithful companions to man throughout the ages. Fossil remains of dogs have been identified from the beginning of the Bronze Age, c4500BC. Throughout time these loyal animals have been used primarily as working dogs. Their purpose was to help humans find or kill animals for food.

Today, dogs are primarily domestic pets. However there are still large numbers of dogs used in the workplace. Their occupations can be as diverse as sniffing for drugs to helping blind or deaf people lead normal lives.

Move this paragraph to ① (A)

Hounds

These are the earliest known working dogs. They tend to be athletic and have a good sense of smell. Well known breeds include the Dachshund, Greyhound, Beagle and Irish Wolfhound.

Gundogs

These are also known as sporting dogs in America. ~~They are very popular in the USA.~~ These were developed to act as assistants to the hunters. Popular gundog breeds include Labradors, Retrievers, Pointers and Springer Spaniels.

Terriers

These dogs were ~~designed~~ bred for tackling burrowing animals such as badgers and rabbits. They usually force the quarry out of its den to be dealt with, rather than kill underground. ~~They are very tenacious animals.~~ Terriers tend to be short-legged, stocky animals that have alert and individual temperaments. Popular terrier breeds include Border and Cairn terriers, Jack Russell terriers and Scottish terriers.

Utility

These are ~~rather~~ a miscellaneous collection of breeds that do not ~~necessarily~~ fit neatly into one of the other categories. The breeds contained in this group are very wide ranging. This category contains breeds such as the ever popular Dalmatian, Chow Chows, Poodles and Bulldogs.

Document 1 (cont)

This section only in single line spacing

Working Dogs

This category includes the working dogs of today. These are often used for police and farm work as well as helping disabled people. Generally very intelligent animals with plenty of stamina, the breeds include Dobermann Pinschers, Rottweilers, Shetland Sheepdogs, Corgis and Collies.

Toy Dogs

do not generally have a working role as such, but

Toy dogs perform a very important role in the lives of the many people who enjoy owning these dogs. As the name suggest, toy dogs are small, companion type pets. They are generally easy to look after and do not require a massive amount of exercise. Popular toy dogs include Yorkshire Terriers, Chihuahuas, Pugs and Pomeranians.

Document 2

Recall this document stored under Dog Display. Amend as shown. Use a ragged or justified right margin. Save as DOG2 and print one copy.

TRAINING YOUR DOG ← Centre this heading

It is very important that your dog is a fully obedient trained animal. This will help ensure the safety of your pet and others. Dogs should be trained to walk to heel without running away or pulling on its lead. They should sit and stay on command.

Spend around 10 to 15 minutes each day on training. If you are in a bad ~~temper~~ mood or short tempered for some reason then do not attempt any training. Use firm and gentle tones to give commands and use your dog's name often. This will attract its attention and make it more receptive to training.

Most dogs enjoy being trained. The secret is to practice little and often. A two hour session will prove boring and frustrating for both of you. The animal's concentration span will not last for very long. The session will only end in tears.
— Emphasise this sentence.

Praise is very important when training. Each time your dog does something well then give the animal plenty of praise. Treats can be used, but a better way is to make a fuss of the dog and show it that you are pleased.

Your dog will ~~learn~~ need to socialise with other dogs which is a very important skill. It is well worth finding out where the local dog training club meets and joining in some sessions. You will learn all about training your pet and meet other owners.

Inset this paragraph 30 mm from left margin

Document 3

Recall this document stored under Dog Table. Amend as shown. Use a ragged or justified right margin. Save as DOG3 and print one copy. Do not rule the table.

FEEDING YOUR PET DOG

It can be very difficult to ensure your pet dog does not overeat. It is very tempting to give them extra treats and scraps. Do not give in to the temptation. Dogs can easily become overweight. This may well have an effect on their heart and they may develop diabetes and other weight related illnesses.

Try to give your dog good quality food and leave out treats and snacks. If you must give treats, for example when training, then reduce the amount of food it has to compensate.

The table below shows healthy weights for various breeds.

BREED	MAXIMUM WEIGHT	GROUP
Shih Tzu	8.1 kg	Toy
Pug	8.2 kg	Toy
Pomeranian	2.5 kg	Toy
Japanese Chin	3.2 kg	Toy
King Charles Spaniel	6.3 kg	Toy
Schipperke	7.3 kg	Utility
Cairn Terrier	7.5 kg	Terrier
Border Terrier	7.0 kg	Terrier
Pekingese	5.5 kg	Toy
Chihuahas	2.7 kg	Toy

Display the GROUP column before the MAXIMUM WEIGHT column eg BREED GROUP MAXIMUM WEIGHT Shih Tzu Toy 8.1kg

Remember, this is only a guide. There are other factors that should be considered such as the build of the animal. If you are in any doubt, contact your local veterinary surgeon.

Examination practice 2 – Document 1

Recall this document stored under DAYS OUT.
Amend as shown. Change to double linespacing
(except where indicated). Adjust the line length to
13 cm. Use a justified right margin. Save
as GIFTS and print one copy

Inset this paragraph 20 mm from right margin

HAVE A DAY OUT

~~exciting~~

Our company offers ~~interesting~~ and unusual days out. You can ✓
choose from a wide range of interests from gliding lessons to
recording your own cd. Enjoy a day doing something you have
always dreamed of, or treat your family and friends.

We also sell gift vouchers which can be exchanged
for any of our events. If preferred, these can also
be exchanged for luxury hampers or flowers. Given
below are some of our exciting treats.

● Gliding lesson. This amazing event gives you the
opportunity to try out gliding over some of the most
beautiful countryside. You will learn how to turn
and manoeuvre the glider during the 30 minute lesson.
A fully trained and experienced instructor provides
expert tuition in a dual controlled glider.

This paragraph in single linespacing

and have prepared the song you wish to sing

Make a Pop Video. Find out if you will be this country's next
pop idol! This day gives you the opportunity to record a track
to cd and star in your own pop video. You should bring your
own backing vocals. Once you are happy with the vocals you
will then record your video using the latest technology to make
your video something special.

Move to point marked ●

discover

Harley Davidson passenger ride. You will ~~find out~~ why Harley
Davidson owners are amongst the keenest motorcyclists in the
world. This event consists of a two hour passenger ride on a
Harley Davidson, driven by an experienced motorcyclist. You
will also have the opportunity to meet other owners and find out
about rallies and shows.

Document 1 (cont)

Firefighting. As a child you may have dreamed
of becoming a firefighter. Now you can make
your dreams come true with our unique
firefighting day. This event is held at a
dedicated fire training centre. You will learn
how to fight fires, use rescue equipment and
breathing apparatus and even deal with a major
incident. You will be trained by a team of
qualified instructors.

Grand Prix Karting Day. This full day event allows you to test your karting skills on a Grand Prix track. Experts will give you individual tuition and you will have the opportunity to try out your new skills in an exciting race. This is great fun for all the family.

three

Weekend Survival Camp. A ~~two~~ day trip into the wilderness where you will learn survival skills. Fully experienced and trained instructors will show you how to keep yourself alive in even the most harsh conditions. You will need to be physically fit for this activity.

(Emphasise this sentence)

For more information on these please call Phoenix Activities on 0807 1212 2882.

Document 2

Recall this document stored under IDEAS.
Amend as shown. Use a ragged or justified
right margin. Save as GIFTS1 and print
one copy.

GIFT IDEAS ← Centre this heading

Are you stuck for an interesting and unusual gift
idea? If so, why not give your friends and family
a special day to remember? We offer fantastic
days out to suit almost everyone.

Our service offers a wide selection of activities that can
be enjoyed by people of all ages and tastes. There
are over two hundred activities ranging from gliding
lessons to learning how to be a secret agent!

Emphasise this sentence

If you are not sure which of the many activities would suit your friends and family,
then buy them a gift voucher. These can be redeemed against any of our activities.
Flowers and luxury food hampers are also on offer for those who do not wish to take a
day out.

The activities on offer are not as expensive as you
might think. A golfing day out costs from as little
as £25. If you have a larger budget then consider
our flying course lessons which costs £5500 for five days.

For a free catalogue call Phoenix Activities or visit our website www.phoenix.co.uk.

All you need to do is request a copy of our catalogue, spend an enjoyable evening
reading about the events on offer and then call us. We will do the rest!

Inset this paragraph 40 mm
from the left margin.

Document 3

Recall this document stored under ACTIVITIES. Amend as shown. Use a ragged or justified right margin. Save as GIFTS3 and print one copy. Do not rule the table.

PHOENIX ACTIVITIES

delighted

We are ~~pleased~~ to announce we have added more exciting days out to our comprehensive list. These are not shown in our current catalogue and so if you would like more information, please visit our website www.phoenixactivities.co.uk or call 0807 121 22882.

These activities will be available from 1 September.

ACTIVITY	PRICE	CODE
Bungee jump	£90	BUNG
Hot air balloon flight	£120	HOTA
Quad bike experience	£130	QUAD
Dragster passenger ride	£180	DRAG
Birds of Prey experience	£65	PREY
Fly a tiger moth	£110	TIGR
Helicopter trial lesson	£500	HELI
Wine tasting	£45	WINE
Catamaran sailing day	£120	CATA
Rally driving tuition	£250	RALL
Hydro zorbing	£160	ZORB
Rock climbing	£50	ROCK
Tank driving experience	£130	TANK

Display the CODE column before the PRICE column

eg

ACTIVITY	CODE	PRICE
Bungee jump	BUNG	£90

Please note that age restrictions may apply to some of our activities.

Examination practice 3 – Document 1

Recall this document stored under Property Article. Amend as shown. Change to double linespacing (except where indicated). Use a ragged or a justified right margin. Save as Property1 and print one copy.

RENTING A PROPERTY ◀ *Centre this heading*

At some point you will want to leave your family home and live an independent life. This might be because you are starting college or working away from home. You may just want to enjoy a house share with some of your friends. *What should you look for when finding a property to rent?*

This section only in single linespacing

determine

First of all ~~work out~~ how much you can afford to pay each week or month. You should look at your net earnings, that is the money you take home each week or month. Aim to spend no more than one third of your earnings on rent. *This is because you will need to have money for utility bills, travel to work, clothes and other expenses. It will not be much fun if you cannot afford to go out in the evenings because the rent is too high.*

Once you have found out how much you can spend on rent, the type of property you can afford will be much clearer. If you cannot afford a one bedroom flat or studio apartment, you will have to consider sharing with friends. *and to have put money aside for when bills arrive*

Although it may seem great fun to share with friends, remember that sharing your living space is very different to sharing an evening out. You will need to ask yourself if you will be able to spend time with your friends day in and day out. Are your friends good at cleaning up after themselves? Would they be responsible enough to pay the rent on time?

You will need to think very carefully about these aspects of sharing. Many good friendships have fallen apart after sharing a house or flat.

Once you have decided who you are going to live with, you need to find somewhere to live. Take your time to look around and find somewhere suitable. One of the most important aspects is to find accommodation near to your work. Travelling long distances can be very expensive and tiring.

If you check that you can afford the rent, and have chosen your flatmates carefully, living an independent life can be great fun. You will also learn a whole new set of skills that will prepare you for adult life.

Move to ✖

Document 1 (cont)

Be realistic about the facilities you require. The more facilities ~~a property~~ has, the more expensive it will be. *the accommodation*

For example, most furnished accommodation will provide the basics such as cooker and microwave for your use. Extras such as washing machines, tumble dryers and dishwashers may not be included.

Document 2

Recall this document stored under Property Display. Amend as shown. Adjust the line length to 12 cm. Use a justified right margin. Save as Property 2 and print one copy.

LANDLORD INFORMATION

If you are an existing landlord or are looking to rent a property, talk to us. We offer a wide range of services that can help you.

Our premier service includes full management of your property. We will find a <u>suitable</u> tenant and manage the let on your behalf. This means that any little problems will be dealt with by us. We will even guarantee the rent for six months in the unlikely situation that the tenant defaults on the rent.

Emphasise this word

The charges for this service are £250 setting up fee, plus 12% of the gross rent.

Insert this paragraph 40 mm from left margin

If you would prefer to deal with the day to day running of the property yourself, then we can help by finding you a suitable tenant. We will check their references and credit history on your behalf. You do not have to pay any fees until an agreement is signed.

The charges for this service are ~~as follows,~~ £125 setting up fee plus £250 introductory fee.

We can also take and check inventories at the beginning and end of tenancies. This is a full professional service and will relieve you of the need to visit the property.

The charges for this service are £250 per inventory check.

accommodation

If you have a ~~property~~ that you would like to rent out, please call us on 01083 10193939.

Document 3

> Recall this document stored under Property Table. Amend as shown. Use a ragged or justified right margin. Save as Property3 and print one copy. Do not rule the table.

PROPERTIES TO RENT

Phoenix Properties is the largest letting agency in Plymouth. We currently have over 50 properties available to let immediately. From one bedroom flats to six bedroom houses we will be able to find something to suit you. Many of our properties are fully furnished.

Listed below are some of the new properties we have had signed to our agency during the past week. If you are interested in finding out more about any of them, please call us on 01803 8482991.

PROPERTY	CODE	WEEKLY RENT
One bedroom flat	FLAZ	£65
One bedroom flat with parking	FFBC	£70
Two bedroom flat	FLDK	£85
Two bedroom flat with parking	FBUS	£95
Two bedroom terraced house	HVLJ	£100
Two bedroom terraced house with parking	HIAS	£120
Three bedroom terraced house	HSLS	£125
Three bedroom semi-detached house	HDEP	£125
Three bedroom bungalow	B.RAV	£140
Four bedroom terraced house	HMEP	£155

> Display the WEEKLY RENT column before the CODE column eg
>
> | PROPERTY | WEEKLY RENT | CODE |
> |---|---|---|
> | One bedroom flat | £70 | FLAZ |

If you have a property to let do contact us. We have a large number of tenants who are actively seeking accommodation. Short and long term tenancies required.